John Matthews has spent more tha[n twenty...] writing about the Arthurian Legends [and the Grail Tradition. An] important aspect of his approach is the value of personal involvement on the part of those who read or study the tradition. He is the author of many books on these subjects and, whilst continuing to explore the work himself, he gives lectures and runs workshops both in Europe and America.

The *Elements Of* is a series designed to present high quality introductions to a broad range of essential subjects.

The books are commissioned specifically from experts in their fields. They provide readable and often unique views of the various topics covered, and are therefore of interest both to those who have some knowledge of the subject, as well as those who are approaching it for the first time.

Many of these concise yet comprehensive books have practical suggestions and exercises which allow personal experience as well as theoretical understanding, and offer a valuable source of information on many important themes.

In the same series

> **the elements of**

the grail tradition

john matthews

ELEMENT

Shaftesbury, Dorset · Rockport, Massachusetts · Melbourne, Victoria

© Element Books Limited 1990
Text © John Matthews 1990

First published in Great Britain in 1990 by
Element Books Limited
Shaftesbury, Dorset SP7 8BP

Published in the USA in 1991 by
Element Books, Inc.
PO Box 830, Rockport, MA 01966

Published in Australia in 1991 by
Element Books
and distributed by Penguin Books Australia Limited
487 Maroondah Highway, Ringwood, Victoria 3134

Reprinted 1991
Reprinted March and August 1992
Reprinted 1993
Reprinted 1995

Reissued 1996
Reprinted 1997

Designed by Jeni Liddle
Cover illustration by Debbie Maidment
Cover design by Max Fairbrother
Typeset by Selectmove Ltd, London
Printed and bound in Great Britain by
Biddles Limited, Guildford and King's Lynn

British Library Cataloguing in Publication
data available

Library of Congress Cataloging in Publication
data available

ISBN 1–86204–033–8

CONTENTS

To
the memory of David Jones (1895 – 1974)
artist and writer
who saw the totality of the Grail.

THE MYSTERIES OF THE GRAIL

The dead King lies in the perilous bed
Uncorrupt, his soul caught in a wrack of air,
His hands folded in a long dream of day.

The Grail Knight, distant, wrought of clay
Dreams of a King whose wounds will never heal
Unless the Cup is brought to birth.

In the silence of the dark earth
The waters stir to life
The King's hands wake and move.

The hands of the Knight eschew strife;
He holds the sword from the red stone
And wields the bonds of love.

The neophytes who watched the sky above
The Castle of the Grail, awake
To see the Mystery complete.

John Matthews

Acknowledgements

To Caitlin Matthews for making the intricacies of *Peredur* sensible to me, for allowing me to ransack the researches for her forthcoming study, *Sophia: Goddess of Wisdom* (Unwin Hyman, 1990) for parts of Chapters 2 and 3. And as always for all her support and love during the writing of this and other books. You're wonderful!

To Gareth Knight for allowing me to use my version of the meditation in Chapter 5, originally devised for a weekend course at Hawkwood College in 1986.

Parts of Chapters 2 and 3 originally formed part of an unpublished manuscript worked on by the present author with Caitlin Matthews in 1982. Grateful acknowledgement is given to her for permitting this material to be used.

Thanks to all those who willingly talked of their own Grail experiences and permitted the inclusion of them within these pages.

INTRODUCTION:
WHAT IS THE GRAIL TRADITION?

LOOKING AT THE MYTH

The Grail Tradition is the embodiment of a dream, an idea of such universal application that it appears in a hundred different places as the teaching of sects, societies and individuals. Yet, although its history, both inner and outer, can for the most part be traced, it remains elusive, a spark of light glimpsed at the end of a tunnel, or a reflection half-seen in a swiftly-passed mirror.

Nor must we forget that the stories which make up the Grail Tradition contain the basic teachings of a Mystery School, its tests, its trials, and its initiations, all hidden within the rich symbolic core of the Grail texts. These are themselves part of a larger Tradition, that of the Arthurian Legends[62], which also constitute the framework of a secret body of teaching.

> The legends of chivalry are veiled accounts of man's eternal search for truth. These beautiful stories are not, however, merely folklore. They are parts of an orderly tradition, unfolding through the centuries and bearing witness to a well-organised plan and program. Like the myths of classical antiquity, the hero tales are sacred rituals belonging to secret Fraternities perpetuating the esoteric doctrines of antiquity[35].

These words, written by the founder of the Philosophical Research Society, Manly P. Hall, sum up as well as one could wish the reality of the Grail Tradition. But there are problems, both of definition and methodology, which must be met with before one can really begin to understand them. Another great modern seeker, Rudolf Steiner, spoke of the difficulty involved in getting the mystery at the heart of the Grail into proper focus. He added that,

> In occult research ... it has always seemed to me necessary, when a serious problem is involved, to take account not only of what is given directly from occult sources, but also of what external research has brought to light. And in following up a problem it seems to me specially good to make a really conscientious study of what external scholarship has to say, so that one keeps ones feet on the earth and does not get lost in cloud-cuckoo-land[81].

All too many Grail seekers have wandered into just such a place, frequently to remain there. It is very easy to follow a seemingly exciting clue into deep waters where the currents run strongly, and to suddenly find oneself out of one's depth. This is in part due to the extraordinary diversity of the Grail Tradition, which this book can do little more than touch upon. But it is also due to a certain 'light-headedness' which tends to come upon the would be seeker. The Grail can bring about extraordinary effects within the individual psyche, as we can see from the personal accounts to be found in Chapter 6.

But it has been open season on the Grail for a long time now – people have been putting forward theories ever since the twelfth century when French poet Chrétien de Troyes left his *Story of the Grail*[13] unfinished and started a trail of wonder which is still being followed. Some of the theories are sensible, some are not. In recent years for example the Grail has been compared to, or identified with, a number of actual cups, bowls, stones, or jewels. It has been described as a container for the Shroud of Turin[17]; as the mysterious Altar of St Patrick[30]; as a Bloodline[38]; and as a sacred relic[1]. People seem desperate to pin it down, to say what it is and where it is. Yet somehow, despite all this, the theorists have managed by and large to keep one fact clearly in mind. The Grail itself, whatever its origins, is somehow special, connected in some way to the idea of spiritual awakening.

The great mythographer Joseph Campbell has a passage in one of his books, which says it all very well:

> It is one of the prime mistakes of many interpreters of mythological symbols to read them as references, not to

mysteries of the human spirit, but as earthly or unearthly scenes, and to actual or imaginal historical events: the promised land as Canaan, for example: heaven as a quarter of the sky; the Israelites passage of the Red Sea as an event such as a newspaper reporter might have witnessed. Whereas it is one of the glories of [the Grail Tradition] that in its handling of religious themes, it retranslates them from the language of imagined facts into a mythological idiom; so that they may be experienced, not as time-conditioned, but as timeless; telling not of miracles long past, but of miracles potential within ourselves, here, now, and forever[10].

The Grail may be all of the things mentioned above – or it may be none of them. It may be something else entirely, something which has no form, or more than one form – it may not even exist at all in this dimension. The important thing is that it provides an object for personal search, for growth and human development, for healing.

In fact, it is more often not the object itself that we are concerned with but the **actions** of the Grail that we seek – the way it causes changes to happen – in the heart, in the mind, in the soul. It is these actions, and the way they came to be recorded, that we shall be exploring throughout this book – and perhaps also learning to work with, if we follow the exercises which are to be found at the end of each chapter.

But to begin with we need signposts. There is no point in simply stepping off into inner space with no idea of what we are looking for. So let us begin with a breakdown of the essential story. This is taken from a number of texts and will not therefore be found within any one account, but it combines most of the elements and gives a broad idea of what we shall be looking at in more detail later on.

THE ESSENTIAL STORY

Some traditions hold that the Grail originated as a jewel – an emerald – from the crown of the Light Bringer, Lucifer, the Angel of the Morning, which fell to earth during the war between the Angels. Others believe that Seth, the child of Adam and Eve, returned to the Garden of Eden in search of a cure for his father's illness, and was given not a remedy for Adam's sickness, but one for the sickness of all men, as well as a promise that God had not forgotten us – the Grail. Whatever theory we choose, the Grail makes its first physical appearance in recorded history at the time of the Crucifixion.

3

The story begins with Joseph of Arimathea, a wealthy Jew to whose care Christ's body is given for burial and who, according to some accounts, also obtained the Cup used by Christ at the Last Supper. While the body is being washed and prepared for the tomb, some blood flows from the wounds which Joseph catches in the vessel. After the Resurrection, Joseph is accused of stealing the body, and is thrown into prison and deprived of food. Here Christ appears to him in a blaze of light and entrusts the Cup to his care. He then instructs Joseph in the mystery of the Mass and the Incarnation, before vanishing. Joseph is miraculously kept alive by a dove which descends to his cell every day and deposits a wafer in the cup. He is released in AD 70, and joined by his sister and her husband Bron, goes into exile overseas with a small group of followers. A table called the First Table of the Grail is constructed, to represent the Table of the Last Supper. Twelve may sit there, and a thirteenth seat remains empty either in token of Christ's place, or that of Judas. When one of the Company attempts to sit in it he is swallowed up and the seat is thereafter called the Perilous Seat.

Joseph next sails to Britain, where he sets up the first church here in Glastonbury, dedicating it to the Mother of Christ. Here the Grail is housed, and serves as a chalice in the celebration of Mass in which the whole company participate, and which becomes known as the Mass of the Grail.

In other versions Joseph goes no further than Europe and the guardianship of the Grail passes to Bron, who becomes known as the Rich Fisherman after he miraculously feeds the company from the Cup with a single fish. The company settles at a place called Avaron (again perhaps, Avalon) to await the coming of the third Grail Keeper, Alain.

A temple is built at Muntsalvache, the Mountain of Salvation, and an Order of Grail knights comes into being to serve and guard the vessel. They sit at a Second Table, and partake of a sacred feast provided by the Grail. A form of Grail Mass once again takes place, in which the Grail keeper, now called a King, serves as priest. Shortly after, he receives a mysterious wound, variously in the thighs or more specifically the generative organs, caused by a fiery spear. Thereafter the guardian is known as the Maimed or Wounded King and the countryside around the Grail Castle becomes barren and is called the Waste Land – a state explicitly connected with the Grail Lord's wound. The spear with which he is struck becomes identified with the Lance of Longinus, the Roman centurion who in Biblical tradition pierced the side of Christ on the Cross. From this time on there are

4

four objects in the castle – the Cup itself, the Spear, a Sword which is said to break in the hands of its wielder at a crucial moment, and either a shallow dish or a Stone. These are the Hallows, the four sacred treasures which must be sought, and wielded, in a mysterious way, by those who seek the Grail. Each of them, in a certain sense, *is* the Grail, which is thereafter said to have five mysterious forms – of which we shall hear more later.

By this time, but only now, we have reached the Age of Arthur, and the scene is set for the beginning of the great Quest. The Round Table is established by Merlin as the Third Table of the Grail (though the vessel is absent). A fellowship of Knights, called the Knights of the Round Table, meet there and are bound by a code of chivalry. At Pentecost the Grail makes an appearance, floating on a beam of light through the hall of Camelot, and each and every person there receives the food he likes best (we may see this if we like as Spiritual food) – whereupon the knights all pledge themselves to seek the holy object.

There follows an extraordinary series of initiatory adventures, featuring in the main five knights: Gawain, Lancelot, Perceval, Galahad and Bors. Of these, and of the many knights who set out from Camelot, only three are destined to achieve the Quest. Lancelot, the best knight in the world fails because of his love for Arthur's queen. Gawain, a splendid figure who may once have been the original Grail knight, is shown in the medieval texts as being too worldly, though he comes close to the heart of the mystery.

For the rest: Galahad, who by a marvellous law of change and substitution is the son of Lancelot and the Grail Princess, is destined from the beginning to sit in the Perilous Seat and to achieve the Quest. Perceval, like Gawain originally a successful candidate, is partially ousted by Galahad, so that while he is permitted to see the Grail – and to use the Spear to heal the Wounded King – at the end of the Quest he returns to the Grail Castle where he apparently becomes the new guardian. Because once the Grail has been achieved in that time, and since it is fully achieved by one person only – Galahad – rather than the whole world for whom it is meant, the Grail is withdrawn – but not entirely, not forever. Perceval takes up residence again in the empty castle to await the return of the Grail, which will thereafter be once again available for all true seekers. (And this is still the pattern today – even if someone were to achieve the Grail right now, it would still become available in the next moment – and so it will continue to be until the end of all things or the final achievement of the great Quest.)

Bors, the last of the three knights to come in sight of the Mystery, to experience the Grail directly, is the humble, dogged, 'ordinary' man, who strives with all his being to reach towards the infinite, and who succeeds, voyaging with Galahad and Perceval to the Holy City of Sarras, far across the Western sea. Of the three, he alone returns to Camelot to tell of what has happened. For despite Galahad's personal success – he looks into the Grail and expires in a transcendent moment of Glory – the Quest has been a failure. Merlin, serving the great powers of Creation, had wished to build a perfect kingdom – Logres within Britain – into which the Grail would come and which would then be transformed into the Holy City on Earth, the Earthly Paradise – from which the whole world would be renewed. As it is, the best that can be achieved is the healing of the Waste Land – a kind of inverse Paradise in ruins – and the Maimed King.

Arthur's realm, the earthly world, suffers from the actions of the Grail rather than benefiting from them. Many of the Round Table knights are killed on their search, or anyway die in the attempt, and Lancelot, his great heart almost broken by his rejection at the very door to the chapel of the Grail, returns to his old love and ushers in the downfall of the Table and of Arthur's and Merlin's dream.

THE TRUE MYTH

Such is the story in its essentials. We are dealing here with high things, with a Mystery that is almost too much for us. But we can learn, and grow, from studying it, by sharing the adventure of the Quest with those far-off people of the Arthurian world, who in truth are not so far off at all. Whatever else it may be, the Arthurian Tradition is first and foremost pure myth. And like all myths it is filled with archetypes. The smallest episode within the huge, rambling edifice may contain enough material to furnish a dozen meditations. And it must be said that this is still the best way of getting 'inside' the stories. Of course we must begin by reading the texts: most are currently available in English, and though there are many of them, each one contains something of value, But once we have become familiar with the world of the great Arthurian forest – that seemingly trackless wilderness through which the Quest knights wander, encountering fresh adventures at every crossroad, bridge or clearing – once we have entered and begun to explore that world for ourselves, then we really begin to understand what the Grail is and why it is worth looking for.

POSTSCRIPT

While I was completing the final stages of this book, I encountered a wonderful example of the living quality of the tradition. The latest, spectacular motion picture of *Indiana Jones and the Last Crusade*[50] opened in London to packed houses. It concerns, basically a modern Grail quest, and adds a new chapter to the myth. Indiana Jones goes in pursuit of his father, who is the greatest living expert on the Grail and who has been taken prisoner by the Nazis. After many adventures the cup is discovered in 'a certain valley in Hatay'. It is a plain wooden cup, which nonetheless heals the mortally wounded scholar, and brings death to the evil seeker after eternal life. Then, it is lost again, in the depths of the earth.

Familiar themes abound. The Grail is guarded by an ancient crusader, one of three brothers whose lives were extended beyond mortal span by the power of the Cup. Images of the Wounded King, the three knights of the Grail, and the power of the vessel to bring either life or death are clearly present in the film. The tradition is thus shown to be as vibrant and living as ever, and for the first time since Chrétien de Troyes is received by a large and rapturous audience!

John Matthews
London, 8 July 1989

PART ONE:
HISTORY

1 · THE CAULDRON OF REBIRTH:

THE CELTIC GRAIL

A FAR OFF BEGINNING

We must look a long way back in time for the origins of what is today understood to be the Grail Tradition. Not for us the panoply of King Arthur and his Round Table Fellowship; we see no shining Cup or radiant maiden, bearing the holy relic through a hall of Medieval splendour. Instead we find an ancient cauldron, intricately carved, its rim set with pearls 'warmed', according to one text, 'by the breath of nine attendant muses'[49]. And this cauldron has the power to grant life, to give forth rich foods, and to bestow upon its owner rare favours. It is possessed by gods and goddesses, it is stolen and stolen again. Hidden and revealed, it lies at the centre of the ancient British (which is to say Celtic) mysteries. And it is sought after as a talisman of power, just as the Grail was to be in the time of Arthur.

Many of the attributes and qualities of the Cauldron are to be found, still present and active, within the later traditions of the Medieval romancers who compiled the vast body of material which became known as *The Matter of Britain*, the stories of Arthur and his knights, and of their great quest for the miraculous Cup.

It is thus to the mysterious realm of the Celtic imagination that we must look for much that is otherwise obscure in the later texts, and in particular to the earliest owners of the wondrous vessel – the

The Grail Procession by Howard Pyle

gods and goddesses, and the heroes who even then had begun the search[54].

THE CAULDRON OF CERIDWEN

Of all the God or Goddess-owned cauldrons mentioned within Celtic tradition, one of the earliest and most important is that of the Sow Goddess Ceridwen, one of the most important Celtic deities.

The story goes that Ceridwen had a son named Avagddu, which means 'darkness', who was of such terrible hideousness that no one could bear to look upon him. So the Goddess decided to brew an elixir of pure wisdom and knowledge which would equip her offspring to fare better in the world. She set out to gather the ingredients which would go into the brew, and she set her servants, an old blind man named Morda and a boy named Gwion, to boil her great Cauldron.

The ingredients were gathered and the Cauldron heated. Then Ceridwen went out again, leaving Gwion to stir the mixture. While she was away however, three drops flew out of the Cauldron and scalded Gwion's finger. Automatically, he thrust the finger into his mouth and thereby gained all knowledge, for the three drops were the distillation of Ceridwen's brew.

At once Gwion was aware that the Goddess knew what had occurred, and that she was coming after him in anger. With his newly found powers, he changed his shape to that of a hare and fled. Ceridwen changed her shape to that of a greyhound and gave chase. Through several more metamorphoses of animal, bird and fish Gwion fled and the Goddess pursued, until finally in desperation he became a grain of wheat in a heap of chaff. But Ceridwen took the form of a red-crested hen and swallowed the grain. And thereafter she bore a son in her womb and gave birth to him nine months later.

Ceridwen would have killed the child but she saw that he was beautiful beyond measure, and so she put him into a leather bag and cast him into the sea, where he floated for nine nights and nine days until the bag caught in the weir of the Chieftain Gwyddno Garanhir. There it was found by Gwyddno's son Elphin, an unlucky youth, who had lost all his goods and had been awarded the fateful May-Eve catch of salmon which always came to his father's nets on that day. This time however there was no salmon, only a leather bag which squirmed and wailed. And when Elphin took it forth, bemoaning his evil luck, and opened it, he found the child within, and one of his men remarked at once on the beauty of the infant, and especially his broad white brow. 'Taliesin be he called' said Elphin, for the word meant 'radiant brow', and thus he was called ever after. And though he was still but a new born child he made a song for Elphin which was to be the first of many[30]:

Fair Elphin, dry thy cheeks!
Being too sad will not avail,
Although thou thinkest thou hast no gain
Too much grief will bring thee no good;
Although I am but little, I am highly gifted.

Weak and small as I am,
On the foaming beach of the ocean,
In the day of trouble I shall be
Of more service to thee than three hundred salmon . . .
There lies a virtue in my tongue
While I continue thy protector
Thou hast not much to fear.

Thus was Taliesin, Primary Chief Bard to the Island of Britain, born of the Goddess from the child Gwion. He became the greatest bard of the age, and went on to prove himself a powerful magician and prophet in the tradition of Merlin, whose successor he became when the great enchanter withdrew into the Otherworld. But all his power came from the Cauldron of Ceridwen, and the three drops of inspiration which he had accidentally imbibed.

This is an ancient tale, and an even older theme. We may believe without fear of contradiction that it hides an ancient initiatory experience, in which the candidate was given a drink containing elements to send him into a visionary trance in which he saw past and future events and was put in touch with the *awen*, or inspiration, becoming at once a poet and a prophet. The nature of the transformations, into bird, beast and fish, indicate the shamanic nature of the experience, since all shamans were taught to discover and identify with various totem animals, who became their guides and helpers in the inner realms, whence they travelled to learn the secrets of creation. Taliesin's story is one of the clearest we possess of this initiatory sequence, and the present author has written elsewhere at length on its profound meaning[60].

Elsewhere the theme appears in the story of the famous Irish hero Fionn MacCumhail, who in his youth was set to catch the Salmon of Knowledge for his master Fintan, and when he has done so, is given the task of cooking it. Then, as he lifts it from the fire to give to Fintan, he burns his thumb on the hot flesh and thrusts it into his mouth just as Gwion does in the story outlined above. Fionn too learns thus the power of animal and bird speech, and can read the future by putting his thumb into his mouth and biting upon it.

The salmon was long recognised by the Celts as a bearer of wisdom; surely such a long-lived creature, who knew how to find its way back to its spawning grounds, could only be a symbol of the gods. Therefore to eat of its flesh was to partake of the nature of the Divine, just as Taliesin does by being reborn of the Goddess.

The idea of placing the thumb or fingers into the mouth seems to be reflected in one of the few references to Celtic methods of divination of which we have knowledge. This is known as *dichetel do chennaib* which may be translated as 'divination by finger ends' and possibly refers to the ancient, magical language of Ogham, which consisted of numbers of horizontal strokes crossing a vertical line in various combinations. 'Finger Ogham' could be made by using one finger to form the 'stave' and the others the crossing strokes. This was almost certainly used as a method of conveying messages between one initiate and another[59].

Thus in the very first example of the appearance of the Cauldron we see that it gives wisdom, knowledge, inspiration, and the ability to shape change – all necessary aptitudes for crossing the divide into the Otherworld.

THE CAULDRON OF BRAN

The second example of the Celtic fascination with Cauldrons – and one which brings us firmly into the realm of the Grail – is that of the God Bran, whose title, 'the Blessed', indicates in what degree of reverence he was held. The story comes, as does that of Taliesin, from the collection of Celtic wonder-tales gathered together under the title *Mabinogion*[30], which means literally 'tales of youth' or as we might say, 'tales of young heroes'. It contains most of the earliest reference to Arthur and the Grail, as well as an astonishing collection of magical stories unequalled anywhere.

In the story of *Branwen Daughter of Llyr* we find the following account.

Bran the Blessed was King of Britain, and he arranged for his sister Branwen to marry Matholwch, the King of Ireland. At the wedding feast one of his brothers, Evnissien, took slight at the Irish king and mutilated his horses. Strife seemed imminent, but Bran offered Matholwch the Cauldron of Rebirth, into which dead warriors were placed and came forth alive again. Matholwch already knew of the Cauldron which came originally from Ireland and was owned by a giant and his wife, Llassar Llaes Gyfnewid and Cymidei Cymeinfoll, who gave birth to a fully armed warrior every six weeks. They had been driven out of Ireland and had taken refuge with Bran.

Branwen now went to Ireland, where she bore Matholwch a son, but was so unpopular with the people that she was forbidden his bed and put to work in the kitchens. There she trained a starling to carry a message to her brother, who once he heard of her ill treatment came with all his warriors across the sea. Matholwch retreats and sues for peace, which is granted on condition that he abdicates in favour of Gwern, his son by Branwen.

At the feast which ensues, Evnissien again brings disaster by thrusting the child into the fire. Fighting breaks out and the Irish are winning because they put their fallen warriors into the Cauldron. Evnissien then crawls inside and stretching out, breaks both the vessel and his own heart. Bran is wounded in the foot by a poisoned spear and instructs his surviving followers, who number only seven, to cut off his head and bear it with them.

They journey to an island named Gwales, where they are entertained by the head of Bran and the singing of the Birds of Rhiannon for eighty years, during which time they know no fears or hardship and forget all that they have suffered. Then one of their number opens a forbidden door, and at once the enchantment ceases and they remember everything. Bran's head tells them to carry it to London and bury it beneath the White Mount with its face towards France. The seven then return to Bran's country and find it under the power of a magician named Caswallawn. The remainder of the story is told in the next tale in the *Mabinogion*, but does not concern us here.

Here the Cauldron is shown to have definite Otherworldly status. The gigantic man and woman, Llassar Laes Gyfnewid and Cymideu Cymeinfoll can persuasively be identified with Tegid Foel and Ceridwen with whom she is partnered in later traditions. Both are said to come from a lake with an island in the centre and both possess a wonder-working cauldron. We may perhaps go no further with this identification than to say that both couples seem to represent an earlier, more primeval tradition of the Otherworld, connected in some way to the race of aboriginal giants hinted at elsewhere in Celtic mythology. But it is worth remembering that the woman of the pair in *Branwen* is said to give birth to fully armed warriors – which seems itself like another echo of the Cauldron story, where it is seen as giving life to (previously dead) warriors.

We are told that Matholwch soon discovered the mistake he had made by allowing the couple to remain in his court: they had multiplied so rapidly and committed such outrages that in less than four months we find the Irish King trying to be rid of them. They do this by building a huge iron house which is then heated, with the giants inside it, in an attempt to destroy the unwanted guests. This theme seems to originate in an Irish tale called *Borama* where the king is actually called Brandub, which is the probable reason why the story became attached to the story of Bran the Blessed. Once again there is the suggestion of a giant cauldron, in which the giant and his wife were placed in the hope that they would be destroyed. This is reminiscent of certain Alchemical practices which we shall examine in more detail in Chapter 3. Here the alchemical King and Queen are placed in a huge bath which is then heated. They emerge renewed and transformed. The idea is ultimately the same – those placed into the Cauldron of Rebirth, come forth renewed.

In *Branwen*, of course, the giants escape and go to Britain, where they become peaceable citizens. Here, unlike the treatment they received in Ireland, they are made welcome and Bran 'quarters them throughout every part of the kingdom' – a reference no doubt to the breeding properties of the giantess, who appears to provide excellent soldiers for the British army!

And so we move towards the next appearance of the Cauldron. Bran learns of his sister's ill treatment and arrives in Ireland with an army. Negotiations take place and at Branwen's suggestion the Irish king has a hall built for Bran – again perhaps a reference to a giant cauldron? But what occurs then is tragic: Branwen's child is thrown into the fire and consumed, Bran receives a wound in the thigh and in the ensueing battle the Cauldron is brought into play by the Irish to revive their dead. Until, that is, Evnissien, finally regretting his earlier actions, himself gets into the vessel and breaks it – and his heart – in the process.

THE PIERCED THIGH

Meanwhile, Bran has seized Branwen and cries aloud the words which are usually translated as 'Dogs of Gwern, beware of Morddwyd Tyllion'. This is a very important sentence, because although it sounds virtually meaningless in this context, it becomes clearer if one translates Morddwyd Tyllion as 'Pierced Thigh'. This, as we shall see, is a suitable title for Bran. 'Dogs of Gwern' has been taken to refer to the Irish followers of the boy Gwern, who is, however briefly, their king. But if we again translate the word 'gwern' literally, as 'alder swamp', the whole sentence then reads 'Dogs of the alder swamp' (that is, the Irish) beware the Pierced Thigh (that is, Bran).

The importance of this epithet, as applied to Bran, becomes apparent if we look ahead to the medieval Grail stories, where we find the figure known as the Wounded King, who suffers an unhealing wound in the thigh (generally recognised as a reference to the genitals) which is the ultimate cause of the wasting of his lands – a condition which can only be remedied by the coming of the destined Grail champion, who will bring about the healing of both the king and the land. If we also notice that one of the foremost kings of the Grail lineage is named Bron, we may begin to see the extensive links which exist between this titanic figure of Celtic myth and the kingdom of the Grail.

It is at this point in the story of *Branwen* that we come to one of the most important, as well as the strangest, episodes in the entire collection of tales which go to make up the *Mabinogion*. Mortally wounded, Bran orders his surviving followers (who significantly number seven) to cut off his head and take it to Bryn Gwyn, the White Mount, in London, and bury it looking towards France. So long as it remains there, no enemy will be able to invade the island of Britain from that direction.

However, the seven do not take a direct route to London. They make two stops along the way – firstly at Harlech, where Branwen dies, and then at the mysterious island of Gwales, where eighty years passed in feasting and song. During this time Bran's head continues to speak with and entertain the company as though he was still alive, for which reason the period is known as 'The Entertainment of the Noble Head' and the seven men as 'The Company of the Noble Head.'

Both Helaine Newstead[72] and R.S. Loomis[49], both noted authorities, affirm that this episode arises from a misunderstanding of the word *pen*, which can mean both 'head' and 'chief', – the implication being that Bran was present in his entirety during the period of feasting and song and on the journey to London. Certainly Taliesin, who was one of the seven, refers in a poem to singing before the sons of Llyr – Bran and Manawyddan – at Aber Henvellen (the place towards which it was forbidden to look), suggesting that both were in fact alive.

If we accept this interpretation the island of Gwales becomes an aspect of the Celtic Otherworldly paradise, where heroes spent a timeless period in feasting and song, and which is incidentally a clear precursor of the paradisal realms sought by the Grail questers. It is also wholly consistent with descriptions of the island of Caer Sidi, the Feary Fortress described by Taliesin in another poem as:

Perfect is my seat in Caer Siddi.
Nor plague nor age harms him who dwells therein.
Manawyddan and Pryderi knew it.
Three tuneful instruments around the fire play before it
And around its corners are ocean's currents.
And the wonder-working spring is above it
Sweeter than white wine is the drink in it . . .[60]

THE VOYAGE TO HELL

Bran thus becomes a type of the Otherworldly host who feasts heroes in his magic hall, feeding them from an inexhaustible Cauldron which 'will not boil the food of a coward'. We can see another example of this kind of vessel, and incidentally complete the connections of Bran and the various cauldrons with the Grail quest by looking at another poem, *Preiddeu Annwn*, attributed to Taliesin (whom we should remember was present at the Entertainment of the Noble Head, and is himself one of the Cauldron-Born, an initiate of the sacred vessel).

The poem begins thus:

Perfect was the prison of Gweir in Caer Siddi
According to the testament of Pwyll and Pryderi;
No one before him was sent into it.
A heavy blue chain held the youth,
And before the spoiling of Annwn gloomily he sang;
Till released he continues his song.
Three times the fullness of Pridwen we went in –
Except seven, none returned from Caer Siddi.

In Caer Pedryvan, four times revolving,
We came upon the Cauldron of Annwn
With a ridge around its edge of pearls.
By the breath of nine muses was it warmed,
Nor will it boil the food of a coward.
Before Hell's portals lights were burning,
And when we went with Arthur, of splendid endeavour,
Except seven, none returned from Caer Veddwid. . . .

> (from a reconstruction by the author,[68])

We are hearing of a raid on the Otherworld, lead by Arthur, to steal the magical cauldron of Pen Annwn. Once again the word *pen*, head is important. In this case it refers to the Otherworldly King Arawn, who is here a possessor of a cauldron of incalculable power. Clearly, also, as in the Grail quest, the task is not an easy one. Only seven men – the same number, we note, as returned with Bran from Ireland – come back with Arthur. One of them, again, is Taliesin, who tells the tale. And we may note that the description of the caers (castles) through which the heroes must pass in order to reach Arawn's hall, are remarkably reminiscent of the island of Caer Siddi in Taliesin's other song, and like the island of Gwales in *Branwen*. Indeed, the voyage of Bran to Ireland seemed to have been modelled on the *Spoils of Annwn*, and may at one time have contained only this story, before the account of Branwen's adventures were grafted onto it.

THE KEEPERS OF THE HALLOWS

There is strong evidence, besides, for an identification of Bran with Arthur – not necessarily as identical figures, but as two distinct characters who assume identical roles – as guardians of the Land. We have already seen how Bran fulfils this role in requiring that his head be buried beneath the White Mount in London. Later we are told, Arthur had the head disinterred, declaring that none but he should defend the Island of Britain. Bran's name, which means 'raven' is also linked to Arthur, who in folk-tradition is said to have taken the form of a chough, a type of raven, after his death. To this day ravens frequent the Tower of London, which stand on the White Mount, and it is widely believed that if they ever depart the country will fall – which is why even today the precaution is taken of clipping their wings to make them unable to fly!

All of this raises another question. If Bran is not dead on the island of Gwales, and if, as in the suggested earlier pattern of the story, he carried off the Cauldron (rather than Arthur, who tended to assume the attributes of Bran) then this would make him one of the guardians of the 'Hallows', or 'treasures' of Britain, thus placing him in direct line to the Sacred Kings who were the keepers of the Grail – one of which, as we saw, was called Bron or Brons. This would be quite in line with Bran's title *Bendigeid*, 'Blessed', which for someone who was a type of the Wounded Grail Lord would be perfectly appropriate.

Add to this the fact that Bran is elsewhere associated with a magical drinking horn or platter, and we have what were possibly the Treasures of Annwn, brought back by Arthur/Bran to become the foundation of the later Grail stories where the Hallows were the Cup, the Spear, the Stone and the Dish.

The attribution of the word *pen* to Bran would have put the story-teller in mind of other, older stories concerning beheadings and oracular heads, of which there were a number in Celtic mythology (hardly surprising in a race which treated the severed head as a cult object). As it is the fact that the Company were in the presence of Bran's head need not imply that it was no longer attached to his body! An otherworldly feast presided over by Bran could well be the root of a story which was later added to the tradition of the sacred head of a chieftain buried under the White Mount to guard either the land or an object of special significance.

THE HEAD IN THE DISH

There is another story concerning a severed head which brings us firmly into the realm of the Grail myths. This is the story of *Peredur*. It is also to be found in the *Mabinogion*, and though controversy still rages over its actual date and provenance it can safely be assumed to contain material from a far earlier time than the later medieval romance of the Grail written by Chrétien de Troyes[53].

Brought up in woodland seclusion by his mother, Peredur grows up in ignorance of arms. On seeing some of Arthur's knights, he mistakes them for angels. He is soon enlightened and vows to follow them to Arthur's court where he too will become a warrior. His mother gives him misleading advice which causes him to be thought boorish. At court, he defends Gwenhwyfar's honour and rescues her gold cup. After a sojourn with his first uncle where he tests his strength with a sword which breaks and is miraculously reunited again, he meets his second uncle, the Wounded King. Following his mother's original advice, he forbears to ask what is happening when the Grail procession enters the hall. He sees a spear which drips blood and a head floating in a dish of blood but remains silent: an act for which he is later rebuked by the Black Maiden, since, had he asked about it, the land might have been healed along with the Wounded King, but Peredur has, by his thoughtlessness, delayed the day of restoration. In a series of adventures Peredur is enamoured of a beautiful woman, learns arms from the Nine Witches of Gloucester, slays a serpent and gains the ring it guards, overcomes a giant, kills another serpent and wins the gold-granting stone it guards, and finally comes upon the Woman of the Mound, who gifts him with a ring of invisibility which aids him to overcome a third monster.

Peredur is transfixed with love for her but finds himself entering the Otherworld. During his sojourn, he presents himself to the Empress of Constantinople (conceived of as a Faery Queen) and overcomes all the knights in the tournament which she has called. Peredur kills three cup-bearers and sends their cups to his hostess during the tourney – a miller's wife. He then marries the Empress who is none other than the Woman of the Mound who originally helped him. After fourteen years in the Otherworld, Peredur returns to Arthur's court where a Black Maiden comes to rebuke him for delaying the healing of the land. The Grail quest proper begins. During this quest, Peredur comes upon a castle where there is a chessboard which plays by itself. The side Peredur supports loses and he casts the board into a lake. He is forced to retrieve it, since it belongs to the Empress. He has to overcome the monstrous black man, Ysbidinongyl. He then kills a unicorn whose horn is causing the waters to dry up. Finally, he comes to the Castle of Wonders – the Grail Castle – where it is revealed that many characters within the story were Peredur's cousin in disguise. The head in the dish belonged to another of his cousins. Peredur and Gwalchmai, with the help of Arthur, finally defeat the Witches of Gloucester who have caused the enchantments.

Here the object which in Chrétien's version of the story becomes the Grail, is a dish, and instead of containing holy blood, or spiritual food, it contains a severed human head – that of Peredur's cousin whom he seeks to revenge. Although at one level this turns the story into a quest for vengeance, we must not forget the Celtic obsession with the human head, which as we saw in the story of Bran became an object for reverence which magically provided food and entertainment for the whole company – just as, later on, the Grail was to do for the company of the Round Table.

Other talismanic objects abound in this story: the ring guarded by the serpent of the mound; the ring given to Peredur by the Woman of the Mound; the ring he takes from the Maiden of the Tent; the cup stolen from Guinevere and later restored to her; the magical chessboard won from Ysbidinongel; the unicorn's head won by Peredur for the Empress; and of course the Spear Which Drips Blood and the head in the dish, which is seen but not won by the hero.

This list can be matched with the list of the Thirteen Treasures of the Island of Britain[58], which tradition ascribes to the guardianship of Merlin, on an island not unlike that in both the *Spoils* and *Branwen*. For a full and detailed discussion of the intricate relationship of these items to the Grail mystery the reader is referred to *Arthur and the Sovereignty of Britain* by Caitlin Matthews, especially Chapters 7 and 9.

For the moment we need to look more closely at the idea of the otherworldly island on which the Hallows are kept, and which provides us with further analogies with the story of the Grail.

THE FORBIDDEN DOOR

We are told in *Branwen* that on the island of Gwales the Birds of Rhiannon sang to the company, and that as long as no one opened the forbidden door that looked towards Aber Henvellen, then all would be well. The Birds of Rhiannon belong to the Goddess of that name. They are of the kind that sing so sweetly that those who hear them no longer notice the passage of time or feel any sorrow or fear. That these are otherworldly sirens is clear, as is the fact that it is they rather than the presence of Bran's head which keeps the company in a state of suspended life. There is a very close analogy of this episode in the later medieval text of *Perlesvaus*, in which the heroes visit the Island of Ageless Elders.

They looked beneath a tall tree with branches spreading wide, and saw the clearest and most beautiful fountain that any man could describe. . . . Beneath the fountain two men were sitting,

22

with air and beards whiter than new-fallen snow, yet their faces seemed young indeed[6].

They go into a wonderful hall and there see:

> The richest tables of gold and ivory [they] had ever seen. One of the masters sounded a gong three times, and into the hall came thirty-three men, all in one company; they were dressed all in white, and each bore a red cross on his chest; and they all seemed to be thirty-two years old. (ibid)

When this company sit at table a golden crown on a chain descends from above, and a pit is opened in the middle of the hall: '. . . the moment the pit was uncovered, the greatest and most lamentable cries ever heard rose up from below; and when the worthy men in the hall heard them they . . . began to weep.' (ibid) What happens to put an end to the idyllic life? In *Perlesvaus* the wondrous hall is built above a pit of lamenting souls. In *Peredur* one of the company, Heilyn son of Gwyn the Old, decides that he cannot rest until he knows what lies behind the Forbidden Door. The result we already know: the Company remember their former lives and the sorrows they had experienced, and immediately set out for London to inter the head of Bran.

All of this seems like a clear parallel to the Christian Fall. The knowledge which comes from opening the forbidden door, like that which comes from eating of the fruit of the tree of Good and Evil, is the same, sorrow and dismissal from Paradise. Yet this is part of the lot of humanity, that they should not remain in paradise so long as that means remaining in ignorance (even though protected) of the true state of Creation.

In this Celtic version, instead of the angelic guardians of Eden, there are the Birds of Rhiannon, spinning a dream around the heroes so that they forget themselves. But there is a built-in fail-safe, which is *already known to Bran* before even the seven set out for Gwales with the miraculous head. In the text Bran *tells* them they will remain for an exact number of years (eighty) and this is shown to be the case. Bran must also know the nature of the magical birds. Was it they who were imprisoned behind the forbidden door, so that when it was opened they flew away? Perhaps they should also be seen as Branwen's birds, comparable with the tame starling who carries a message to her brother?

Far more is intended to be understood by the opening of the door than we are told in *Branwen*. It is a doorway between worlds which is opened, one which allows for passage both ways, between this world and the other, of those who dwell in either place. In setting Bran's head to watch over the land of Britain from the White Mount, there is also a sense in which the inner archetype of Bran is placed in a position of guarding the otherworld as well – the exchange taking place by way of the door – which we must remember we are not told is *closed* again after the departure of the seven, only that it was opened.

THE ISLAND OF WONDERS

Another, later, text, makes the symbolism even clearer. *Sone de Nausay*[49] is a medieval story, but as is often the case it contains material from significantly earlier sources. Here we find related the adventures of the brave knight Sone, who takes service with the king of Norway. Most of the story is not relevant to our present exploration, but one episode is of vital importance for the clues it offers both to the identity of the island of Gwales and its place in the Grail mysteries.

In order to receive the grace necessary to overcome a gigantic warrior, Sone and Alain travel to a mysterious island named Galosche, where they find a beautiful castle with four towers at each of the four corners and in the centre a great hall. This castle is curiously inhabited by monks, who however, possess two wondrous relics: the uncorrupted body of Joseph of Arimathea and the Grail itself. . . . These are shown to Sone and the story of the vessel retold. Long after, Sone returns to the island to be married and is permitted to carry the Grail in procession, with the Spear, a piece of the True Cross, and a candle which had been carried by the Angel of the Annunciation!

The description given here of the Island of Galosche (Wales? Gwales?) is typical of the Grail castle and the turning island and the four-cornered city in *Preiddeu Annwn*. But there is so much here that bears a resemblance to episodes in *Perlesvaus* that one might be forgiven for believing they shared a common source. Both texts describe a collection of paintings depicting the Annunciation and the Harrowing of Hell. In both, a coffin containing the body of a great man, in this case Joseph of Arimathea. And both texts contain a description of a land under the curse of barrenness, though here it is Logres rather than the Island of Need which is in question.

The Substitution of Joseph for Bran in *Sone* is possibly due to a misunderstanding on the part of some unknown copyist of the word *cors*, which while it can mean body, also means horn. We remember that Bran was the possessor of a remarkable horn; when this was read as body it would have been natural for the medieval writer, who knew

24

the Grail story, to replace the pagan god with the figure of Joseph, whom he probably mistook for the wounded King, retaining the image of Bran's wound at the same time.

The seven followers of Bran have become twelve in both *Sone de Nausay* and *Perlesvaus*, where there are twelve monks and twelve ageless elders respectively. But we can still see the influence of the earlier story in the ageless men in the latter text, as we can also see echoes of the sorrowing Company of the Noble Head in *Branwen*, in the weeping and wailing monks in *Sone*, and the sorrowful sounds emanating from the pit on the island of Ageless Elders.

In the *Historia Meriadoci*[18], a thirteenth century romance written in Latin, we find the island of Gundebaldus, which is square, lies at the centre of a bog and is only connected to dry land by a narrow causeway (elsewhere this becomes the famous Sword Bridge leading to the Castle of the Grail). There are four castles on this island, as there are in the *Preiddeu Annwn*, and in the centre is a beautiful hall with gardens. The hero, Meriadoc, meets the wizard Gundebaldus on the causeway and fights him, successfully knocking him into the bog. The name Gundebaldus has been identified as a variant of Gwynas or Gwynn, another name for the King of Annwn. The name of the fictitious king of Norway in *Sone* is given as Alain, a name also attached to one of the later Grail kings, and which may well be a corruption of Arawn, the owner of the Cauldron in *Preiddeu Annwn* . . .!

In the Celtic wonder-tale *The Voyage of Maelduin*[58], there is another island, divided in four by walls of precious substance: gold, silver, copper, and crystal, and each quarter allocated to kings, queens, youths, and maidens respectively. These refer to the four elements and the four directions on the shamanic Wheel of the Year, and on each of the four quarters of the island can be placed one of the four ancient Hallows of the Grail which first appear in their Celtic forms as: The Stone of Fal from Falias; The Spear of Lugh from Gorias; The Sword of Nuadu for Findias; and The Cauldron of the Dagda from Murias.

THE PLACE OF THE FOUR HALLOWS

From all the above we arrive at a picture. It is of an island four square, perhaps made of glass or crystal according to other Celtic sources, divided in four or with four towers or castles at each corner. At the centre is a mysterious enclave surrounded by a wall or fence that is difficult to penetrate. Here the Grail is sometimes to be found, and all who sit down at its table are fed with the food they most desire. In some mysterious way this is the heart centre of both land and people, even though it is often situated on an island off the coast of the mainland.

Here all things are balanced and there is no hardship or anger, fear or hatred or dread. In fact the paradisial realm of the Grail. It is possible to make a glyph of this:

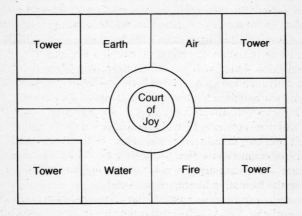

Figure 1: The Blessed Realm/The Realm of the Grail.

Here the four directions/elements meet in harmony. Add to this the shape of the Grail cup in its more abstract design, and we arrive at a mandala of the Grail, where all things meet and are balanced, where the aspirations of humanity meet the desire of God to be reunited with His creation.

This image is reflected almost universally, whether it be in one of the marvellous mandalas of the mystic Hildegard of Bingen, or a Hopi Indian sand painting, where the power of the four directions is recognised. Here we see the reconciliation of head and heart, the balancing of male and female, the above and below, the placing of the four Hallows on the Table of Creation, and the Elements in the Divine Cauldron of Time and Space.

THE SLEEPING TITAN

When the Company of the Noble Head return to Britain, they find that time has moved on. The seven men left behind to guard the kingdom have all been overthrown and killed, including Bran's son. Caswallawn, son of Beli, now rules over the land. There is again a sense that just as there is an inner and outer Bran, so the seven men left behind are somehow surrogates for the seven who were present at the Entertainment of the Noble Head. There is, too, an echo of the episode we looked at from *Perlesvaus* where Arthur, absent from the land, is thought to be dead and other events take their course as though he were indeed no longer ruling.

Caswallawn, the new ruler, is presented as an infamous magician, who slew six of the seven guardians while wearing a cloak of invisibility. Caradac, Bran's son, broke his heart at the sight of his friends falling to an invisible opponent. There is a strong echo here of the later episodes, which will be dealt with fully in Chapter 4, where the knight Balin, staying at the castle of the Grail king, sees a knight struck down by the king's invisible brother. Though Balin does not die of grief, his reaction, the slaying of the invisible attacker, does bring death and destruction in its wake, and his own death follows shortly.

The Company is, in a very real sense, without its 'head'; Bran is buried in the land as its new palladium. He thus joins a select group of figures whose importance must be recognised for the part it, too, plays in the formative history of the Grail.

It has already been suggested that Bran shares enough common factors with the Grail king to substantiate his identity as a prototype of the Maimed King. His guardianship of the Cauldron, and ultimately

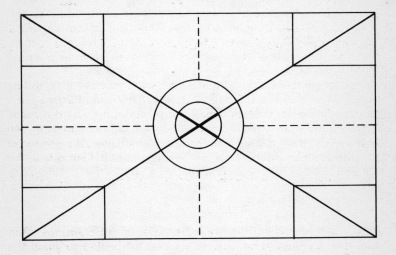

Figure 2: The Mandala of the Grail.

of Britain, further identify him as a type of *genius loci*, such as Arthur later became, sleeping beneath the land until he is needed to reaffirm his lordship. Another such figure, from Classical mythology, who shares these attributes, as well as Bran's gigantic stature, is Cronos, the father-god of the Greeks. If we turn to Classical literature and to a text by Plutarch, which has often been quoted to show how Britain was seen as an otherworldly realm by the rest of the ancient world, we get a vivid picture of the buried God. The quotation comes from a work entitled *The Silence of Oracles*[75] which tells how a Greek named Demetrius visited Britain to investigate the island's religious traditions.

'There is' he says, 'an island there where Cronos is a prisoner guarded by Briarius in his sleep – sleep was the fetter devised for Cronos, and many daimons lie around him as servants and followers.' This is further amplified in *The Face of the Moon*[75], also by Plutarch, where it is said that:

> The natives [of Britain] have a story that in one of these [islands] Cronos has been confined by Zeus, but that he, having a son as a gaoler, is left sovereign lord of those islands . . . Cronos himself sleeps within a deep cave resting on rock which looks like gold . . . birds fly in at the topmost part of the rock, and bare him ambrosia, and the whole island is pervaded by the fragrance shed from the rock. (ibid.)

Not only is this astonishingly reminiscent of descriptions of the aged Grail king kept alive by a host brought to him by a dove from heaven, but it also establishes clearly the nature of the sleeper and reminds us as well of the island on which Bran resides, with the company of the Noble Head and the Birds of Rhiannon.

In Greek myth Cronos is the last of the Titans, who having castrated his father Uranus, becomes lord of the world. He later consumed all the children of his wife Rhea except for Zeus who finally overthrew him and chained him in the Islands of the Blessed. He is thereafter seen as ruling over a lost Golden Age much as Bran (also 'the Blessed') during the feasting of the Noble Head. Both are shown as sleeping beneath the land, guardians of the door between the upper realm and the otherworld. Arthur joins them as the latest in a line of guardians – the Pendragons, the Chieftains of Annwn – who await the call to come forth from their magical sleep and defend their country.

All of this throws a new light on the idea of the Grail kings and their origins. They are a part of the legacy of Celtic tradition which helped shape the future development of the Grail myths, and which are felt throughout most of the medieval retellings which followed. For something like five hundred years these and other stories continued to circulate, first in Britain and later in Europe. Eventually, they returned, christianised and shaped anew, but with the same underlying elements still perceivable beneath the layers of new material which had been grafted upon them. We shall see something of what occurred in the next chapter.

EXERCISE 1: THE COMPANY OF THE NOBLE HEAD

Close your eyes and sinking deeply into meditation, prepare to embark on a journey. Visualise before you this scene: a low-lying level plain, with long grass waving in the gentle breeze of midsummer. Above you the sun is high in a clear blue sky. Ahead see a low mound, scarcely a hill, almost certainly man-made. In the centre of the side facing is a door made of two mighty upright stones capped with a huge lintel. As you approach great wooden doors fold inward on noiseless hinges. Within, all seems dark, but as you go forward you see a dim light which grows brighter the further you go, until you find yourself at last standing in what seems to be a long hall, high-ceilinged, supported upon huge timbers carved with intricate spiralling designs. As you look about you see that the walls themselves seem to be of wood, and that everywhere they are carved in reliefs depicting scenes of people hunting, of warriors battling and drinking, of men and women making love. . .

In the centre of this great hall burns a great fire, casting a warm red glow over everything, flickering across the walls, so that the carved figures seem to move. . . . Around the fire pit are benches and tables, arranged in a rough circle, and, as you watch, the hall, which had seemed empty, begins to fill up with people. Proud, fine-boned men with strong, fierce faces, many sporting long moustaches: slender fair women, some with hair unbound, others with plaits reaching below the knee. All alike are dressed in bright colours: brilliant reds and blues, deep greens and startling yellows.

You notice three in particular who stand out from the rest, who sit upon ornate chairs where the rest throng noisily onto the benches. These are two men and a woman; the men both handsome and dark-haired, the woman, who might be their sister, white-skinned as the moon, with dark, red hair and keen, far-seeing eyes. She it is who now looks towards you, and beckons you forward. You are invited to join the company, to sit on one of the benches and room is made for you.

Once you are seated, liquor is brought round, a foaming brew served in rough leather tankards. It tastes somewhat like cider, but with a deep sparkling freshness which leaves you feeling more alive after you have drunk it.

Now you see a figure step forth into the firelight: a tall slender man dressed in simple green. He carries a small harp and round about his brows is a fillet of silver which glows like starlight. As he begins to play you are entranced, for the music seems like the most sweet and lovely sound you have ever heard. You may feel tears starting to your eyes as you listen, but you are aware also that the eyes of the harpist are upon you, and that his cool gaze looks deeply into you, reading all that is there to see . . .

As you listen to the music of the harpist, you lose all sense of time. You have perhaps sat there for only a few moments, or maybe far, far longer, when at last you become aware that the music has ceased, a new element has been added to scene. Across the room from the three carved chairs you see a huge, wise and gentle head. It is as though it is floating there, yet there is nothing fearful or repellent about this; the face is so filled with joy and merriment; the eyes brimming over with life, the lips smiling . . .

After a moment of complete silence, when even the bright throng of men and women have fallen completely still, you hear again the sound of the harp, and now a voice is raised in song, high and sweet and more pure than anything you have ever heard. At first you cannot quite hear the words, but slowly you realise that the song is coming from the mouth of the Noble Head, though it seems to be made up not of one voice, but of many. Gradually you begin to pick out the words and to realise that what is being sung is meant directly for you and you alone. Although all who are present listen with such attention that maybe all hear something which is of particular significance to them.

Listen carefully and try to remember what you hear. . .

At length, the Great Song is ended. If you have listened with heart as well as ears, you will have learned much that will be of help to you in the months and years ahead. For you are now one of the Company of the Noble Head and once you have heard the Song that is sung you can never wholly forget it. As you look the great face slowly fades from sight and you find yourself once again in the great wooded hall beneath the green mound. It is time to depart and sadly you take leave of the bright gathering. As you rise from your place and return the way you came, you notice that on three sides of the hall are great wooden doors securely barred and bolted. The wood from which they are made seems more ancient than that of the rest of the hall, blackened and weathered by countless fires burning in the great hall. You may wonder about the doors later on and one day you may return to see them opened . . .

Now as you return the way you came, the light begins to fade and you see before you the archway of the door by which you entered. Outside is bright sunlight, but when you step through the doors you find that it is the cold light of midwinter. You have been within the mound for a full half year.

Slowly now let the scene begin to fade from you and become aware again of your surroundings. In your own time re-establish contact with the world around you. But always remember what you learned in the Hall of Blessed Bran.

2 · CHRIST'S CUP:

THE CHRISTIAN DIMENSION

A NEW DIMENSION

By the late twelfth century the stage was already set for a new epiphany of the Grail. The Middle Ages had achieved their first flowering: a springing forth of new ideas and beliefs in minds freed at last from the sheer effort of survival. Art, architecture and literature were in their vernal aspect; Chartres cathedral was still under construction, and complex webs of theology and mysticism were being unwound in both monastery and university. The relationship of mankind with creation, and with God, were amongst the all important questions of the age.

Despite, or perhaps because of the fact that literacy was a skill reserved almost exclusively for clerics, memory was correspondingly stronger than today. The ear, not the eye, was the gateway to the imagination; when it came to storytelling, there were always willing listeners to wonder-tales in which a semi divine hero slew beasts and overcame implacable enemies in order to rescue and eventually marry, archetypal maidens.

There was also a stronger sense of conceptual or symbolic understanding. Labourers were known by their implements of toil, religious by their habit, nobility by their rich apparel, knights by their mounts and weapons. Although the liturgy of the Mass was in

32

Latin, except perhaps for the sermon, which may have been in the vernacular, this did not seem to matter; the actions of the priest at the altar were necessarily mysterious, emblematic of the way in which he mediated between heaven and earth on behalf of the congregation.

Factors such as these helped prepare the way for the return of the Grail, as did the political state of Europe at this time. Prior to the spread of Christianity the whole of the Western world had been torn apart by war and insurrection; orphaned from its Classical roots by Barbarians who eventually made the West their own homeland, Europe remained a tangle of petty kingdoms, each one battling for supremacy.

Each kingdom, however small, had its own capital. The archetype for these capitals was, religiously, Jerusalem, the city of the Divine King; mythically, it was Camelot, the stronghold of the Earthly King, Arthur of Britain. And indeed, the role of kingship within European society was a significant one: kingship sprang from a divine source as it had from the Goddess of Sovereignty in Celtic times, and kings were annointed with oil just as priests were – emphasising the priest-like nature of the office.

This descent of kings from a divine source was of the greatest importance to medieval man. We must remember that Europe was a wilderness of forest and trackless waste, partitioned by rivers and lakes and still very much under the influence of tutelary gods and goddesses. Each tree, hill and well had its guardian spirit; standing stones, circles and sacred groves retained a sense of the numinous. Although only folk memory of these things survived, the king had to be a consort of the gods as well as the people if he was to wield any power.

It is this which makes the idea of the Wounded King, which we saw springing from Celtic myth, such a powerful theme within the Grail cycle. The wounding of the king caused the wounding of the land because of the deep and indissoluble links between them. Its presence within the Arthurian stories demonstrates how thin was the veneer of Christianity upon the original beliefs of the West. The power of Rome had not yet assumed the extremes which resulted in reformation and counter-reformation, but few had the strength to step outside its laws.

The further the influence of the Church spread through Europe, the more exoteric became its expression. Yet even within such strictures, the real message of Christ managed to survive; a body of mystical and esoteric teaching was upheld by isolated people: mystics, solitary madmen, who were either ignored, lauded as exemplary members of the Church, or if their doctrines attracted undue attention, summarily dismissed as heretics.

It is perhaps significant that there are no 'Grail Saints', no officially approved expositors of what might be termed the Grail 'school' of mysticism, any more than there is either specific recognition or denial of the Grail itself. There is merely a deafening silence which, in an age of relic-hunting, is itself as telling.

THE NEW CORPUS

Almost the entire corpus of Grail literature was written between 1170 and 1225, appearing suddenly and ending almost as abruptly. We can only guess at the extent of oral tradition behind their composition. Certainly the Arthurian canon was already established well before the twelfth century, deriving its roots from the Celtic sources discussed in Chapter 1. Story-tellers such as the trouvères, wandering singers and poets who were able to cross all boundaries, both physical and religious, fused the pagan and the Christian ethos with Chivalric achievement and folk culture, forming an archetypal world which lived in the imaginations of all kinds of people.

Two authors who may be seen as helping to establish the canon of the Grail were Chrétien de Troyes and Robert de Borron. Chrétien was already famed throughout Europe for his Arthurian poems, in which he had introduced such originally Celtic figures as Lancelot, Gawain and Geraint to a Norman French, courtly society who were hungry for more. The Matter of Britain, as it was known, became all the rage, with countless new stories appearing all the time. Chrétien's last work, left unfinished at his death, was *The Conte Del Graal* or Story of the Grail[13], in which he told of the adventures of a young, innocent youth named Perceval, who happened to catch sight of two knights – whom he took for angels – in the forest where he had been brought up in ignorance of all manly pursuits. From this moment he desired only to follow them and to discover where and how they lived. He met many adventures on the way, but the strangest of all was that of the Grail.

Finding himself at the Castle of his uncle the Fisher King, Perceval witnesses a mysterious procession in which a vessel called the Graal is born through the hall and is used in some way to sustain a wounded man. Perceval, either from politeness or ignorance, fails to ask the meaning of these things, and finds himself outcast to wander in the wilderness of the Waste Land as a result. A hideous damsel chides him for his failure and tells him that had he asked the required question the land and the king would have been restored. Thereafter the foolish youth has to suffer in the wilderness for some time before he finds his way back to the castle; but the outcome is never revealed since the poem breaks off before the mystery of the Grail is explained.

The enigma of this story touched the imagination of the Western world, expressing feelings that were already latent within the consciousness of Medieval man. A Swiss knight named Robert de Borron, who may have already been working on a Grail text of his own prior to Chrétien, took the story back through time to the days when Christ walked the earth, telling how Joseph of Arimathea, who gave up his own tomb to contain the body of the Crucified Messiah, had given into his keeping, by no lesser person than Jesus himself, the Cup of the Last Supper[64].

Other writers, notably Wolfram von Eschenbach, whose *Parzival*[92] brought in much of the Orientalism to be discussed in the next chapter, and the anonymous authors of *The Elucidation*[22], the *Didot Perceval*[78] and the vast compilation known as the *Vulgate Cycle*[56] added to and strengthened both the Arthurian background and the mystical dimension.

The dangers of such rival interest was not lost upon the Church which, perhaps in the interest of survival, did its best to exclude troubadours and other story-tellers from communion on the grounds that they were agents of the devil. Eventually, the Church itself took over the office of story-teller; texts such as *Perlesvaus* and the *Vulgate Cycle* were both written down by Cistercian monks who incorporated the uncanonical writings of earlier writers to produce a version which, though it suffers at times from a heavy moral underscoring, yet expresses one of the finest and most complete visions of the Grail to date.

It was these writers who first introduced the figure of Galahad, the stainless, sinless knight destined from birth to succeed in the Quest for the Grail. Yet, he was the son of Lancelot, the strongest physically of all the Arthurian knights, and yet possessed of a fatal flaw – his love for Arthur's Queen. The anonymous author of the *Vulgate Quest*, perhaps seeking a way to Christianise the overt Paganism of the earlier Grail texts, brought about the birth of Galahad by having Lancelot tricked into believing he was lying with Guinevere, when in fact the lady in his bed was the Grail Princess.

One writer has described this as 'one of the greatest moments of imagination ever permitted to man', adding that:

The absurd nonsense that has been talked about [Galahad] being 'unhuman and unnatural' misses altogether the matter of the mystically enchanted fatherhood . . . where the Princess of the Grail abandoned her virginity and Lancelot was defrauded of his fidelity, so that the two great Ways [of Camelot and Carbonek] might exchange themselves for the begetting of Galahad[90].

The author (or compiler) of *Perlesvaus* added a further strand of veracity to the claims made for the myth, telling us that:

The Latin text from which this story was set down in the vernacular was taken from the Isle of Avalon, from a holy religious house which stands at the head of the Lands Adventurous; there lie King Arthur and his Queen, by the testimony of the worthy religious men who dwell there, and who have the whole story, true from beginning to end[6].

The 'holy religious house' mentioned here is meant to be Glastonbury, where the supposed bones of Arthur and Guinevere were discovered in 1184. Also there are the 'worthy religious men', the Benedictines of Glastonbury Abbey – though whether they indeed had 'the whole story' is a matter for speculation.

What is interesting is that both the Isle of Avalon, a recognised name for the Celtic otherworld, and the holy religious house, stood 'at the edge of the Lands Adventurous'. It seems that even the monkish chroniclers recognised that the Archetypal world of the Grail and the Arthurian heroes stood at one remove from everyday life, accessible not only in legend but also physically.

The spate of texts continued unabated. Chrétien's *Story of the Grail* now boasted four continuations, by different hands, which extended and detailed the original by thousands of lines. Robert de Borron had completed his trilogy: a *Merlin*, a *Joseph d'Arimathie* and a *Perceval*[64]. Versions of these stories began to appear throughout Europe, drawn now into the whirlpool of Arthurian literature. Descriptions of the Grail and of the mysterious procession, some based on Chrétien's original version, others displaying a degree of originality, appeared in Germany, Italy, and Spain[26]. The mighty *Vulgate Cycle* was begun, perhaps to give a more authoritative Christian stamp to the material.

THE OLDEST CHURCH

Yet another strand in the strange and wondrous history of the Grail was its part in the division between Rome and the so called Celtic branch of Christianity. Robert de Borron had connected the Grail with Joseph of Arimathea, and had brought his Saintly hero to Britain along with the Grail. Here he had founded the first church in these islands, substantially *before* the Church of Rome and with the apparent warrantry of both Christ and his mother. In more than one Church Council thereafter British Bishops claimed the right to prior speech before those of other countries, solely on account of this early ascription of Christianity to Britain.

The Wattle Church

Celtic Christendom was discouraged and secretly considered heretical by Roman missionaries, who found it well established when they arrived in the first century. Even after the Synod of Whitby in AD663, which established such matters as the tonsure of monks and the date of Easter, all was not as it might have been between the different professions. Monks and clerics of the Celtic rite were rarely considered for high office within the Church.

But it was within the boundaries of Celtic Christendom that the stories of the Grail arose. We have to look at the wonder voyages of monks like St Brendan, written in Latin in the ninth century, to see the tendency among such Celtic monkish scribes. The *Navigato Sancti Brendani*[58] is rife with elements which might just as well have come from an Arthurian or Grail adventure: the bold adventurer who goes in search of God's mysteries, treasure, beautiful maidens, monsters, islands shimmering in the seas of the West – the Lands Adventurous indeed.

Such writings as these were the product of a solitary, hermetic existence, suited to the isolated island bothy rather than the community life as witnessed in Benedictine or Cistercian houses. It is perhaps significant that Palagius, a fifth century theologian and exegete, whose doctrine was that man could take the initial step towards salvation by his own efforts, and apart from Divine Grace, should also have originated in Britain. There has always been something sanguine in the British make-up which has not reacted well with the Augustinian doctrine of Original Sin, and we may see in the Grail Tradition this same yearning towards independent salvation – for the meaning of the Grail seems to have little to do with the established means to such an end.

Is it possible that the Grail legends share in the accusation of heresy levelled against Pelagius? It has been noted before that: '. . . its [the Grail's] effects upon those who see it are made to correspond closely with the effects of Holy Communion upon communicants'[16]. Which may explain why the Grail seekers found it necessary to go on quest for something which was ostensibly to be had daily on every altar in every church in the Christian world. But there is something deeper than this yet. The seeker was looking for a level of mystical experience demonstrably *not* present in the fundamental teachings of the Church.

THE INNER LIFE

The basis of the Christian mystery teaching is that it consists of a series of initiations into the life of Christ himself, a sharing of his experience within the compass of our own. We have only to look at the course of Perceval's life within the earlier Grail texts, especially that of Chrétien, to see the parallels which exist there.

Perceval, like all Christians according to accepted dogma, is in a state of sin – his innocence, his ignorance, does not preclude his share in the collective sin of mankind. The Fall, according to Origen[16] occurred because the Beginning [of Creation] was unstable, and unstable because it was innocent. The Beginning is dependent upon redemption through the action of the Apocatastasis (the Restoration of All Things). Just as Christ had to live through the sacred drama of Incarnation, Nativity; Initiation in the desert (an image of the Waste Land), Active Ministry, and Crucifixion, so the Grail hero has to acquire experience on his quest to abrogate the seeds of his own innocence. Christ thus becomes the divine archetype of the Grail initiate – he is seeded in the Grail womb of the Virgin, he vivifies and translates water in the vessel of Cana; he descends into the waters of the Jordan, taking on him the sins of those whom John the Evangelist has previously baptised; he offers his flesh and blood in the Passover meal to his disciples in order that they might literally 'pass over' into the Promised Land of the redeemed (the Otherworld of spiritual mysticism); he begs that the chalice of suffering be taken from him – but nevertheless drinks it to the dregs; he is buried in a hollow tomb after his essential moisture (blood and sweat) have been collected by Joseph of Arimathea; he is resurrected, going first to harrow Hell in an action which is paralleled by the freeing of the waters in the Grail story.

Perceval, on the other hand, is as innocent as Adam before the temptation. It is not until he has failed to ask the all important question about the Grail procession that he becomes alive to the possibility of suffering and its both evil and redemptive consequences. He is informed, quite bluntly, of the death of his mother – he is himself the instrument of her death. We see in him the Fool perpetually innocent and blameworthy; he is smeared with the same blood as Adam and shares his sin. Like a bystander at the Crucifixion he beholds the Grail and the suffering of the Wounded King yet fails to ask why these things should be so. It is possible that:

> The final answers might have been: 'The Lance bleeds to reveal the hope of salvation', and 'In the contents of the Grail which come to you from God the Father and are served to all Christian folk, lies the source of *caritas*, redemption of sin and the getting of salvation'[84].

Yet, though he is 'witless of the Trinity' in Chrétien, Perceval eventually does succeed in his quest precisely because of his innocence/ignorance. He goes through all the levels of initiation in unknowing imitation of Christ; lead through necessary suffering in order to reach the Paradisial object of his search – the Grail itself.

> For there is a foolishness of the Grail as there is a foolishness of the Cross (I Cor, I, 8–23) and the predestined are 'peculiar' in more than once sense; they are not only different, but God's or the Grail's, own possession[11].

This element of predestination runs through all of the Christian Grail texts. It is evident that Perceval, and after him Galahad, partake more closely than the common run of humanity in the mysteries. Perceval's unusual ignorance of even the basic tenets of faith set him apart from the experience of the Medieval Christian in search of salvation. Yet for all that he comes nearer than the great 'worldly' knights, Lancelot and Gawain who, though schooled in the ways of Christianity, turn away and reject the inner life for its outer rewards.

THE TWO WAYS

That wise and astute commentator Joseph Campbell recognised in the dichotomy which runs throughout the whole of the Grail corpus a reflection of a similar disharmony within Christendom itself. Taking the text of Wolfram von Eschenbach's *Parzival* as exemplar he notes:

> This calamity [the wounding of the Grail King Anfortas], in Wolfram's meaning, was symbolic of the dissociation within Christendom of spirit from nature: the denial of nature as corrupt, the imposition of what was supposed to be an authority supernaturally endowed, and the actual demolishment of both nature and truth in consequence. The healing of the Maimed King, therefore, could be accomplished only by an uncorrupted youth naturally endowed, who would merit the supreme crown through his own authentic life work and experience, motivated by a spirit of unflinching noble love, enduring nobility, and spontaneous compassion[10].

This seeming dichotomy was present even at the most profound level, in the nature of the Eucharistic sacrament which played so profound a part in the mystical imagery of the Grail. Christ was God: yet he was also man. His nature was heavenly: yet he was also of the earth. The bread and wine, before consecration, were merely bread and wine: afterwards they became the actual body and blood of Christ, although they remained – in appearance – bread and wine.

Just as the early Church laboured to define the nature of Christ, so the Medieval Church sought to define the nature of these things. The precise definition of transubstantiation, as the miraculous change was termed, was not outlined until the Lateran Council of 1215 – at exactly the time when the Grail texts were appearing. Pope Innocent III merely confirmed what everyone knew; there was reason to be semantically precise, because heresy had begun to threaten the fabric of Christianity at this time. Indeed, heresies which denied the mystery of transubstantiation, preferring more rational explanations of the

Eucharistic sacrifice, existed side by side with an almost talismanic belief in the Real Presence of Christ in the species of Blood and Wine.

The daily miracle of the Mass occurred on the altar in every church and chapel, so that the mystery became familiar without losing any sense of its numinosity. Lay-folk in the West were not protected from the divine mysteries by an iconastasis screen, as was the custom in the East, but were actually encouraged to see them taking place – to the extent that the priest elevated the consecrated gifts while the deacon rang the sacring bell to draw their attention to it. In *Perlesvaus* it is at this moment that Arthur witnesses the Grail's most profound mystery – though in a totally different manner to the normal Mass: '. . . looking towards the altar after the preface, it seemed to him that the hermit was holding in his arms a man, bleeding from his side, bleeding from his hands and feet and crowned with thorns'[6].

In both the Vulgate *Quest del Saint Graal* and later in Malory's *Book of the San Greal*, we come across similar events, in which the Grail heroes, or Arthur, witness an actual appearance of Christ. These texts go out of their way to exhibit a similarity between the actions of the Grail and those of the Eucharist.

That this was in itself unusual is evidenced by the fact that at this point in time (eleventh century), the laity did not frequent the sacrament of Communion in order to receive it. It was not until 1215 that the faithful were obliged to make confession and receive the sacrament at least once a year. Nor did they, even then, receive it in both kinds (bread and wine); this was generally forbidden the laity as the danger of spilling the Precious Blood was considered too great. Kings *heard* Mass before battle, before breakfast, before going hunting – but they seldom received the host; only the priest made his Communion.

THE RESERVED BODY

This makes the actions of the Grail all the more unusual, and leads us to consider another interesting practice. The consecrated bread was, from earliest times, reserved in a box called an *aumbry*. This happened not only within churches but in private houses as well, where the faithful would administer the sacrament to each other in default of priest or deacon, or during times of persecution. The reservation of the sacrament is an intrinsic part of the Grail legends and is mentioned specifically in a translation into Medieval English of Robert de Borron's *Joseph*. In the episode in question Sarracynte, the wife of Evelach of Sarras, one of the earliest Grail Kings, relates how her mother kept the

host in a box, being a Christian secretly for fear of her pagan husband.
Each day she washes her hands and,

> The box anon she opened there;
> Out of the box there issued anon
> Our Holy Saviour in flesh and bone
> In form of bread . . .
> . . . with many tears and sore sighing
> There received she that holy thing. . .[1]

Shortly after this she dies, charging her daughter to keep the box hidden
safely. (Another example of the way in which women seem to have been
the bearers of the Grail mystery while the men were its guardians.)

With regard to the Grail legends it is interesting to note that some
churches are known to have possessed pyxes (receptacles for the
reserved host) in the shape of doves. These were kept over the altar.
In Wolfram's *Parzival*, on Good Friday,

> . . . one can infallibly see a Dove wing its way down from heaven.
> It brings a small white Wafer to the Stone and leaves it there . . .
> from which the Stone receives all that is good on earth of food and
> drink, or paradisial excellence[92].

The stone mentioned here is the Grail, and we shall have more to say
of its significance in the next chapter. Doves seem to have a special
significance within Grail symbology. Again in *Parzival*, we see the
dove as a symbol of hope – the Grail knights see the turtle doves
embroidered on the robes of the hag Kundrie, who is the emissary of
the Grail. They proclaim with evident joy:' Our trouble is over. What
we have been longing for ever since we were answered by sorrow is
approaching us under the sign of the Gral'[92].

REWARDS OF THE JUST

The Grail castle, whilst not in the generally accepted sense a church,
is clearly the focus for sacramental devotion. Its occupants are the
guardians not only of a great treasure, but of a life-giving secret.
The qualities of what is contained in the Grail inspire awesome
joy or reverent dread, and their effects vary from nourishment to
the prolongation of life or the gift of death.

The earliest texts still speak of the Grail in almost Celtic terms as a
cauldron of plenty which nourishes the hungry with their favourite

food, while the sick are healed by a stroke of the sacred Lance. It is not until the later versions of the story that we begin to hear tell of kings suffering mysterious wounds, who are sustained only by a wafer.

In *Parzival* the death of the wounded Anfortas is a release, for while he beholds the Grail he cannot die. Yet again, in Malory, the death of Galahad is the apotheosis of his achievement on earth. At the end of his journey he attends a Mass of Our Lady which is served by Joseph of Arimathea himself in the likeness of a Bishop.

> And when he . . . had done, anon he called Galahad, and said to him, 'Come forth the servant of Jesu Christ, and thou shalt see that thou hast much desired to see'. And then he [Galahad] began to tremble right hard when the deadly flesh began to behold the spiritual things. (52, Bk.XVII. Ch.22.)

Galahad receives the sacrament from his hands and says: 'Now Blessed Lord, would I no longer live'. . . . 'Now wottest thou what I am?' said the good man . . . 'I am Joseph of Arimathea, the which Our Lord hath sent here to thee to bear thee fellowship.' (ibid.) Galahad kneels in prayer and then expires, his soul born to heaven in a manner visible to both Bors and Perceval who remain on earth. Here is one of the central Grail mysteries: it gives life and death, joy and suffering, because it is a vessel, an empty vessel capable of being filled by anything. These great mysteries are indeed akin to that of the Blessed Sacrament; they express, in archetypal terms, the means of salvation and the way to Paradise[61]. But they are mysteries of which it is not meet to speak or to exhibit to the credulous, and thus they are hidden, secrets indeed. It is not without reason that they are guarded by the Grail keepers who, from Joseph of Arimathea to Perceval and beyond, have kept watch over them and passed them down to each succeeding generation.

THE MYSTERIES OF THE GRAIL

These, then, were the sacramental mysteries around which the life of Medieval Christendom revolved. Christ was present among men, not just in the reserved host on the altar, but also in each person who partook of the sacraments. This realisation is an important one. People did not frequent the sacrament in order to be 'good' in some perfunctory manner, but in order to be at one with Christ – in communion. This was, and is, the ultimate aim of every Christian – to be in oneness with God in the person of Christ, whether on earth or in heaven. But the obstacles to this union must be overcome. Man suffers the effects of Original Sin, a loss of sanctifying grace, brought about through Adam's fall. Thus the Grail knights had to struggle against overwhelming odds, always supported and aided by their faith and by the presence of the Holy Hermits who peopled the forest of adventure through which they rode in quest of the miraculous vessel.

The Redemption, whereby man is saved from sin and death, was seen in various ways. In the West, emphasis was given to the expiation of sins through the sacrificial death of Christ; while in the East, the Greek fathers were more concerned with the restoration of man to Divine life – an idea referred to by the term *theosis* or God-becoming. It is a delicate idea to comprehend, and one which the Western Church has understated again and again. Not so the Eastern Church, in which it remains an article of faith.

THE JOURNEY OF SETH

Such intricate webs of symbolism are the underpinning power of the Christian Grail legends. In the great compilation of Biblical legends known as *The Golden Legend*[1], Adam sends his son Seth to seek for the Oil of Mercy with which his father can be cured of age and death. Seth returns with seeds from the Tree of Life which he buries with his father; the Tree sprouts, eventually growing into that from which the Cross on which Christ is crucified comes to be made. The sin of the first Adam is thus redeemed by the second, and symbolically the Tree forms a bridge across which the whole of humanity can pass from death to life.

According to another tradition Seth returns with the Grail, a promise to mankind of the Saviour who will come. While in the *Queste del Saint Graal*, Perceval, Galahad and Bors make their way to the Holy City of Sarras, on a boat made from wood taken from the same Tree. When Galahad lies upon the great bed within the ship he emulates Christ. The ship itself is the Grail knights' way to theosis, the path to God.

AN ALTERNATIVE WAY?

Throughout the Grail corpus there is a thread of independence and individuality which was sufficient to brand it with the taint of heresy. In its literary form it may even have presented a dangerous alternative to the available avenues of Christian fulfilment. Later it was to become associated with the military Order of the Knights Templar and with the heretical Cathars. Both movements were to be stamped out in bloody purges.

The fact that the Grail is housed in the castle of Corbenic, which can be translated as meaning 'blessed or transfigured body' is not without significance. Did the Grail offer an alternative way to salvation? Is this the reason why, to answer an earlier question, the knights embarked on a quest for something which could ostensibly be gained by worshipping daily at the sacrament of the altar?

Perhaps the answer is that the Grail legends symbolised man's personal search for perfection; not a narrowing of sights and a cramping of style, but a generous impulse which could not be contained within the straight ways of orthodox belief. The Church had already begun to develop into an administrative organisation concerned with political, as much as religious, motivation. It had established an exoteric mode of expression.

But, when a received tradition begins to petrify in this way, losing its original cutting edge of truth in a tangle of dogmas, it becomes time for an esoteric tradition to arise by which the great truths may not perish but be revivified and transmitted to further generations. When the established hierarchy fails in its duty, it is as though the angelic powers inspirit humankind to produce those who will continue them. These are the people who stand in direct communication with the will of God: the mystics, who interpret the inner workings of creation; the story-tellers, who realise the truths in popular manner; and the heretics, who delve into forgotten or half-forgotten lore, who formulate alternatives to established ways of belief.

Each of these categories can be seen to have influenced the growth of the Grail legends in one way or another. They can be viewed as simple Christian allegory, as straight forward story, or as rank heresy, according to the prevailing tone of the time. Yet there were those who found no dichotomy in such matters, and it was they who kept the idea of the Grail alive throughout the Middle Ages.

There were those who made their own investigations, reaching conclusions which they could speak of only in code. The source was perhaps as unexpected as anyone could have imagined. For a new and profound influence was about to be brought to bear on the formulation of the Grail legends – that of the Orient, in the shape of Islamic teachings brought back from the Crusades.

EXERCISE 2: JOURNEY TO THE GRAIL LANDS

The country of the Grail is really that of the soul but that is itself a place not often frequented nowadays. Not entirely a Wasteland perhaps, but a place where the weeds are grown tall and the paths tangled. If we are to approach the place of the Grail ourselves we may choose to follow in the steps of the Quest Knights, who set forth to journey from Camelot to Sarras; or we may choose to follow our own path. Either way we need signposts.

There are, if one likes, two important points on the path – the A. and the Z of our journey. Point A is our place in the real world, point Z is Sarras, the Holy City of the Grail where all who join the Quest one day hope to arrive. Between these two points stretches a vast divide – a land peopled with beings both wondrous and strange, many of whom are able to help you on your quest. Indeed we should never think as wasted the time we spend in inner colloquy with the folk of the Grail – they can save us many an hour spent in journeying down paths that lead nowhere. This can be done through meditation on one of the many characters to be met with in the texts.

But what are the best methods of gaining access to the Grail country? Perceval sets out, as do many of the Arthurian knights, knowing nothing of the Quest, nor even why the Grail should be sought at all. So, more often than not, we also tend to set out unprepared. How many reading these pages have already set out, fired with enthusiasm, but without *really* comprehending what is entailed?

So we need to begin by considering what our reasons are, what need we are answering as we set out on this long journey. It is like any magical work, which needs to be contemplated and interrogated before it is begun to make sure that there is no intent to seek power or riches or to cause harm to others. Once these things are sorted out, we are in a much better frame of mind and preparedness than before.

The next stage comes with the realisation that we have to make our own maps – there are none printed for us, no 'X marks the spot' where the Grail is to be found. We might select certain episodes from the texts to offset this, meditating upon them until they are firmly established in our own inner world. It is no good simply saying: 'Right, I'm going to meditate on the Grail now.' You might get some interesting and valuable insights, but you are unlikely to get very far on the journey. And the journey is every bit as important as the final goal.

So, take an episode like Gawain's visit to the Chessboard Castle, where the hero arrives at this mysterious dwelling and finds it apparently deserted. On entering he finds a chessboard set up for a game, and when he moves one of the pieces finds himself matched with an invisible opponent. When he is soundly beaten he tries to throw both board and pieces out of the window, but a woman rises from beneath the waters of the moat and challenges him with the failure of his quest and sets him a further series of tests designed to help him on his way.

There are a number of points here on which we could dwell at some length. Who, for instance, is the mysterious dweller in the moat, who seems to know all about Gawain and his quest? And what is the purpose of the magic chessboard? By the time you have answered these questions – and others which will occur to you – you will also have come to know a good deal more about the Grail Castle and its inhabitants, as well as their function within the Grail country. This gives a signpost to which you may return on your next journey into the world you have come to explore.

Another method of working would be to visit one of the Castles mentioned in the texts which have no specific symbolic attributes (Joyous Gard or Tintagel for instance) and to build the image of this over several days of meditation (it can be based on memories or pictures of any castle – this will not detract from the inner reality of the image). When you have successfully completed this part of the exercise you should climb to the top of the castle and look out at the surrounding countryside. You may be surprised how much there is to see, things of which you were hitherto unaware of.

In this way you can build up a quite detailed scenario of the country, and you will soon begin to notice another surprising thing – the land will not always bend to your will; your imagination will not always shape things as you might wish. In fact it will begin to impose itself on your own visualisations, to become 'real' in ways you might never have guessed could happen. From here on you can make further explorations, charting a course through new territories, finding new places or people not necessarily mentioned in existing texts.

Finally, when you feel you are ready, set out consciously to reach Sarras. How will you journey? By ship? By horse? On foot? What sort of country will you pass through? What, or who, will be there when you arrive? The journey may take time but if you persevere you will almost certainly reach there in the end.

3 · THE STONE OF WISDOM:
ORIENTALISM AND THE GRAIL

The unique quality of European Christianity did not long remain unmixed. Just as it had come to establish itself and was even beginning to seem tame, the rallying call went out through the Western world: 'Aidez le Saint Sepulchre' (Save the Holy Sepulchre). The city of Jerusalem, long seen as an image of heaven on earth, demanded rescue from the Infidel. It was the beginning of a great and powerful movement, which swept up just about every able-bodied man in Europe and flung them headlong into a venture which was to take them into strange lands. Out of this was to come a new strand in the story of the Grail, which went with the Crusaders in their dreams and their literature, and returned, once again transformed.

So far we have dealt with the Christian and Celtic faces of the Grail Tradition. Now, like true Crusaders, we must venture into the realm of Islam. The third of the so-called religions of the Book – the others are Christianity and Judaism – Islam spread quickly throughout the Middle East, eventually encompassing Egypt, Morocco, Spain, Persia and India. It brought with it a new culture as well as a new religion. In medicine, arithmetic, astronomy, geography and philosophy, it led the world: Islamic scholars had access to major Greek writings long before the West – in fact, it taught the West. We shall examine the element of Alchemy, which has a strong bearing on the Grail texts, later; this too had many proponents among the Moslem world, as we shall see.

NOW RECK I NOT THOUGH I DIE·FOR NOW I HOLD ME ONE OF THE BLESSED MAIDENS OF THE WORLD·THAT HATH MADE THE WORTHIEST KNIGHT OF THE WORLD

The Ship of Solomon by Ann Alexander

Jerusalem had been in Islamic hands for a long time before the beginning of the Crusades. Pilgrimage to the Holy Land was possible, if hazardous, under the Abbasid caliphate; but towards the end of the eleventh century the balance of power changed; under the new Fatimid dynasty, permission to enter Palestine seemed doubtful. It was no accident that Pope Urban II should put up the cry for Crusade in 1095. His motivations may have been politically oriented – he desired above all to see the incipient split between Eastern and Western Christendom, Constantinople and Rome, healed, but he also expressed goodwill and a genuine concern that the Eastern Church should suffer while the Western stood by and did nothing to help its brothers in Christ. He therefore proclaimed at the Council of Clermont that to those who would fight to protect Eastern Christendom from pagan incursions, and go onward to liberate the holy places, he would grant general absolution and remission of sins. To those who forsook their promise, he vowed excommunication.

Urban's clarion call opened the way for Christians to perform their duty in clear and unambiguous terms; he managed, unknowingly, to call into being the best fighting force Europe was to see until the Second World War, and at the same time helped to solve the problem of unfocused strength. It had not been long since Christian armies had been persuaded not to fight with each other without good reason, and some areas of Europe still faced the problem of armies fighting across their fields.

The situation can be neatly paralleled by Arthurian tradition. When Arthur came to the throne he had first to prove his supremacy in battle over the rival kings of Britain. After he had done this he engaged their services in policing the country. But when all the fighting is done, when there are no more bold, bad barons to discomfit, no more black knights hoving at fords, and when all the dragons are dead, then the famous Round Table Fellowship begins to be lethargic and to exhibit some of the traits they are vowed to overcome. Then, as the whole court is teetering in the balance, when the scandal of Lancelot's illicit passion for the queen is about to break, the Grail appears, leading to new and wondrous opportunities for growth and adventure.

So, too, the Crusades appeared at the right moment to harness the combined strengths of Christendom into a single spearhead of power. Unfortunately, the parallel holds good when we come to look at the course of the Crusades: great deeds were achieved, but great evils unloosed as well; those who approached the Grail quest unworthily may well have wreaked worse damage than if they had stayed at home. In the Arthurian Tradition the appearance of the Grail heralds the ultimate break-up of the Round Table; so too we must view Urban's call to Christendom, for it undoubtedly set up a chain reaction which we still feel today. Ownership of the Holy Lands, the division between Catholic and Orthodox churches, and many other issues which still trouble us may be seen as originating with the Crusades.

THE CRUSADER CUP

The chief object of the Crusader armies was to liberate the Holy Sepulchre, in the same way that the goal of the Quest Knights was to seek the Grail. But a problem soon emerged: when the Crusaders finally beheld Jerusalem in 1099, there was not a dry eye in their ranks. Hardened killers wept at the sight of their

God's tomb, which was, after all, merely the temporary resting place of Christ's body prior to the Resurrection. The dilemma had still not struck them. The tomb was empty; their victory hollow. It was not until the leaders of the First Crusade began supervising the removal of bodies from Jerusalem, whose streets had been purged of every last Moslem, Jew and, for that matter, some Christians sympathetic to Islam, that they began to wonder – what next?

Christendom retained its tenure in Jerusalem until 1187, when it once again fell into Moslem hands. But, just as no one can appropriate heaven as a personal possession, neither could the Crusaders establish an earthly city as a heavenly enclave. It was not long before wrangling began; religious and secular leaders were chosen, after long dispute, and a kingdom of Jerusalem created, known as Outremer. It remained a bone of contention as claimants came thick and fast on the death of any king careless enough to leave doubtful successors.

The Crusades brought many changes to Christendom. Coffers were emptied to send forth vast armies of men who returned to find themselves homeless. Disillusioned by fighting and religion, they roamed through Europe, begging for food or forming themselves into gangs who terrorised the land. The strengths of Christendom were found to have their weaknesses also; the holy images were blackened by smoke and slaughter. All save one – the Grail, which instead of being weakened by the souring of the great enterprise, seemed to be strengthened.

Chrétien de Troyes, who as we saw wrote the earliest known Grail text, *Le Conte du Graal*[13] was himself in the service of one of the most renowned Crusading families, that of Philip of Flanders, who Chrétien declared had given him the source for his poem from a book he had obtained in the Holy Land in 1177. This date certainly tallies with Philip's movements at the time, and even if he did not bring back an actual text, he could certainly have carried home an account of several sacred objects discovered by the Crusading armies.

Among these was the Sacro Cantino, a green glass dish about 40cms across, which was found during the sack of Caeserea in 1101 and carried by the victorious troops to Genoa, where it remains in the cathedral to this day. It was believed to be the gift brought by Sheba to King Solomon, and to have been made of emerald (sic!). Archbishop Jacapo da Voraigne, writing in the late thirteenth century, gives a first hand account:

That vessel is made in the likeness of a dish, whence it is commonly said that it was the dish out of which Christ . . . ate at the Last Supper. . . . Now whether this be true, we know not; but since with God nothing is impossible, therefore we neither firmly assert nor deny it. . . . This, however, must not be passed over in silence; that in certain books of the English it is found that, when Nicodemus took down the body of Christ from the Cross, he collected His blood . . . in a certain vessel of emerald miraculously presented to him by God, and that vessel the said English in their books call *Sanguinalia*[26].

THE STONE FROM HEAVEN

This is still not quite the Grail, but it is near enough to it. The description of the cup as an emerald is also worth noticing. As such it appears in another major Grail text, the *Parzifal* of Wolfram von Eschenbach[92], possibly the most intricate and symbolically loaded of all the versions – and the one most clearly indebted to Eastern ideas. Wolfram, indeed, claims that he took the essence of his great poem from a book by one Kyot of Provance, who in turn had it from an unexpected source: an Islamic teacher named Flegitanis, who was wise in the wisdom of the stars and who wrote of the great war in heaven between the angels. Lucifer, whose name means, significantly, the Light Bringer, and who had not then been associated with the Christian idea of the Devil, wore in his crown a great emerald. At some juncture, either during the fighting or in his fall from the height of heaven, this became dislodged and, according to Flegitanis, as reported by Wolfram, fell to earth, where it became known as the *Gral* or Grail. Unlike all the other versions of the story, where the Grail generally takes the form of a cup or dish, Wolfram makes it a stone. In *Parzifal* he describes it thus:

A stone of the purest kind . . . called *lapsit exillas*. . . . There never was human so ill that if he one day sees the stone, he cannot die within the week that follows . . . and though he should see the stone for two hundred years it [his appearance] will never change, save that perhaps his hair might turn grey[92].

This description has given rise to a great deal of speculation ever since the work appeared. The Latin is inaccurate and cannot be translated exactly. It may be that Wolfram meant to write *lapis lapsus ex caelis*, stone fallen from heaven, which would certainly square with the story of its falling from the crown of Lucifer. Other interpreters have felt themselves to be on the right track by identifying Wolfram's 'Gral' with the *lapis philosophorum*, the Philosopher's Stone which is the central image for the Alchemical Great Work. This is born out somewhat by the following quotation from the work of one of the greatest of the Alchemists, Arnold of Villanova, who in his work on the *lapis*, written not long after Wolfram's poem, writes:

Hic lapis exilis extat precio quoque vilis
Spurnitur a stultis, amartur plus ab edoctris.
(This insignificant stone is indeed of trifling value,
It is despised by fools, the more cherished by the wise).

The concept of the stone's lack of worth is typical of the symbolism of alchemy, which went out of its way to hide the true meaning of the Great Work in a cloud of impenetrable symbols used in an endlessly changing pattern. The real nature of Alchemy is not, as so many people have been lead to believe, a form of early chemistry in which the Alchemists sought to turn base metal into gold. The element with which they worked was called the *prima materia*, the 'first material', and was indeed more concerned with the human spirit than with the earth, mud, spittle and faeces (among other ingredients!) which supposedly made up the recipe for the creation of the Philosophers Stone.

Working with the element of the spirit they sought rather to transmute *this* into heavenly gold, to perfect Creation, and especially man. This is, of course, very much a function of the Grail, which transforms those who go in search of it into spiritual beings. Christ himself addresses the Quest Knights in Malory's *Morte d'Arthur* in words which make this clear:

My knights, and my sergeants, and true children, which be come *out of deadly life into spiritual life*, I will now no longer hide myself from you, but ye shall see now a part of my secrets and of my hidden things. . . (Bk XVII Ch 20. My italics.)

Alchemy is about 'exchange' and 'transformation'. As in the Grail legends there has to be a meeting point between the Divine and Human, the former reaching down as the latter reaches up. The nexus point of meeting is the Centre, the World, the pivot of the cup shaped Grail. The stuff of humanity, thus encountering the matter of divinity, is transformed. Galahad, as we saw, looks into the Grail and is transfigured into another realm. Arthur, at the end of his first tenure on earth, as Malory says 'changed his life'. Thus in Alchemy, which is a far too vast and astonishingly rich subject to deal with in these pages, the baser elements of humanity are transformed into spiritual gold. Man himself, in the guise of every individual seeker, becomes the *lapis philosophorum*, the *lapsit exillas*, the 'fire-tried stone' which is renewed and set in its rightful place in the crown of heaven.

> Alchemy is fundamentally involved with a mystery; and, though it is not identified so simply as saying it is the mystery of life itself, and man in this place of creation, it is almost that mystery. It is that mystery not in the abstract but as an ongoing series of exercises man must carry out in order to fulfil a destiny his mere existence, his 'magical emergence' from sperm and egg in uterus, already fulfils[31].

The *lapis* remained only a stage in the creation of the Great Work, just as the Grail itself is but a symbol of the interior quest for human perfection and oneness with God. To those who came across Alchemy for the first time its strange and often bizarre symbolism seems to have struck a deep chord. It is possible that Wolfram encountered it in the writings or conversation of one of the many travellers returning from the East – especially the Spanish city of Toledo, where Moslems, Jews and Christians rubbed shoulders in uneasy truce, and which became a veritable melting pot for the teachings and beliefs of the major faiths.

It may have been here that certain concepts of the Judaic mysteries entered into the story of the Grail. Certainly there are recognisable elements of Qabala, that most impenetrable aspect of the ancient mystery schools, from the thirteenth century onwards.

Qabala itself seems to have grown out of a certain difficulty among the Jews in comprehending or entering into relationship with God. Forbidden to mention his name, driven to using synonyms, unable to make a likeness of their deity, the Qabalists evolved a way of coping with the limitations thus imposed upon them not unlike the methods adopted by the Alchemists. They understood God in terms of the Tree of Life, an abstract diagrammatic structure, which allowed symbolism and often anthropomorphic representation of the workings of Creation. While they did not seek to overthrow the accepted tenets of faith, they were lead further and further into areas of speculation about which orthodox Jews were far from happy. They tended, again like the Alchemists, to practice in small groups that kept their activities quiet. But it is from this highly eclectic and secretive source that the next strand of Grail tradition appeases.

THE BRIDE OF GOD

The study of the Qabala (the name means 'from mouth to ear') is based on the revealed Biblical texts and a more shadowy personal revelation which accompanies its exegesis. The Tree of Life represents the plan of God for man – a series of paths and spheres (called Sephiroth) which he must traverse in order to attain union with the Godhead. The journey is the course of life, with all its sufferings and joys, a quest very similar to that of the Grail, but without its Christian bias. As J. C. Cooper notes in *An Illustrated Encyclopaedia of Traditional Symbols*[14], 'The book is connected with tree symbolism and the Tree and the Book can represent the whole cosmos. In Grail symbolism the book can also typify the Quest, in this case for the lost Word.' The paths of the Tree of Life thus offer a multitude of possibilities for every seeker after hidden meaning. The lost Word of the Grail is that uttered by the Solar Logos at the beginning of time, and which will be spoken again at the end. The Grail, like Christ himself, is the Alpha and Omega of creation.

One of the most important mysteries within the intricate system of Qabala is that of the Shekinah, the compassionate Presence of God, who when Adam and Eve were exiled from Paradise, chose to accompany them into exile. This presence of the Shekinah has never been seen by orthodox Jews as a feminine element of the Godhead, but to the Qabalists she was just this, so that they personified her as a woman and as the indwelling soul of Israel – and therefore, of each person. Man is understood as being in captivity, relegated from his perfect state within God but, because he is accompanied by the Shekinah, is enabled to attain it once more. In the same way the Presence of God remains with the Israelites in exile because Moses causes the Ark of the Covenant, which is the 'dwelling place of God' – and therefore of the Shekinah also – to be housed in a sanctuary while they are still pursuing their wandering path through the world.

There is a tradition which says that no one may set out to liberate the Shekinah, or even set out with that intention, because God will choose one to do this, someone who does not know his destiny. This reminds us that Perceval, in the Grail story, does not know his destiny, never in fact intends to seek the Grail when he leases his forest home yet he is chosen, and in all but the latest texts, is the successful candidate.

The Shekinah is also described as the Veil of God, protecting mankind from His awful presence; but she also stands for the Compassion of God. It is she who broods upon the face of the waters when the world is created. She may also be seen as a paradigm for the Grail – the vessel of honour which stands as a covenant for all of God's mercy and richness, a presence to be sought, a love which prompts mystics to journey in perpetual quest until union or realisation is achieved and the world redeemed at last.

In later, Lurianic Qabalism, the concept of the *shevirah*, or 'breaking of vessels' which held the light of God's emanations, was brought about by the lack of harmony between the masculine and feminine elements of the Tree of Life. A similar conclusion may yet be drawn in our study of the elements of the Grail tradition, for the Grail symbolises all that is fertile, liquid, hopeful. It is a totally feminine symbol of God's love which, apart from that of Christ, is noticeably absent from exoteric Christianity. The Grail as Shekinah, as vessel of hope, is not totally without foundation if we look at the parallel examples of the feminine in other religions.

The idea of a feminine counterpart to God, or at least a feminine agency within the Godhead, is too common to be ignored. In Judaism we have seen the Shekinah; within Islam, and particularly within the esoteric tradition of the Sufis, we encounter the Sakina. This form of the word seems to have been taken straight from Jewish sources and adapted to the needs of Islam. It seems to signify angelic withdrawal, a quietude or moment of understanding and bliss such as comes to all who seek the Grail, sooner or later.

Islam also knew of the Gnostic figure of Sophia, the Bride of God, and made use of the symbolism she afforded. For this figure permeated the whole of Western civilisation, beginning with the Platonic world-soul, which in time became inextricably linked with the idea of Wisdom personified as a woman, and thus spread into other forms of belief. The Shekinah, as we have seen, was implicit in Jewish mystical understanding, as was the person of Wisdom as help meet of God in the Biblical books of wisdom. In early Gnostic thought, as this grew up within the Fertile Crescent and interfaced with the ancient Classical Mystery religions, Sophia was considered to be a divine emanation, one of the causes of creation and of the redemption. The early fathers of the Church rejected this idea, deploring the dualism suggested in such a theory. Thus the idea of a compassionate, feminine force descending from the Godhead was neglected.

Despite this, the figure of Sophia and her function became associated with the actions of the Holy Spirit – as though this was itself a feminine aspect of the creator – in Christian iconography represented as a dove. It is thus significant that the dove has always represented a feminine, maternal watchfulness who is seen as 'deploying her strength from one end of the earth to the other, ordering all things for good' (The Book of Wisdom 8.1.). We must not forget, either, that the dove is the symbol of hope to the Grail guardians in Wolfram's poem; and that in the same work the Grail messenger, Kundrie, comes to announce the Lordship of the vessel to Parzifal, dressed in a hood of black samite, on which 'gleamed a flock of turtle-doves finely wrought in Arabian gold in the style of the Grail insignia'[92].

The feminine quality of the Grail is more than apparent in the section of *Parzifal* in which this reference appears. Ferefiz, Parzival's half brother, is a pagan and, because of mixed parentage from Europe and the East, is pied white and black. The Grail is born among the company and Ferefiz announces that he sees no Grail, only an *achmardi*, a word generally used to describe the cushion on which the sacred stone is carried, but which also has the meaning of an emerald, thus linking the Grail further with the stone from Lucifer's crown. Ferefiz is transfixed, not by the Grail itself, but by its bearer, Repanse de Schoye. He is willing to be baptised so that he may marry her.

Repanse appears to have all the attributes of the Shekinah – she bears the vessel of love for all mankind; she shares the sufferings of humanity so that 'her looks have suffered'[92]; she wears the crown of sovereignty or wisdom, like the queen of Israel, or the Queen of the Sabbath in Jewish tradition. Of all the company, only Ferefiz recognises her quality, and desires to marry her. In the baptism which follows, the significance of this salvation and transformation is shown when the font, tipped towards the Grail, miraculously fills with water.

From this union of West and East comes a line of Grail kings, of which more will be said in Chapter 4. We see in her the union of pagan and Christian, black and white, male and female: a cosmic mystery of such importance that it transcends the esoteric and exoteric and reunites them in a primal unity. It is the completion of a strand of the Alchemical Great Work, and it shows the Grail as Divine Sophia, symbolising the ability of man to regain paradise by means of her help.

THE WAR BETWEEN LOVE AND FAITH

Another strand of history which had a most profound effect on the history of the Grail, and which likewise drew its strength from Eastern sources, concerns the history of two groups of people who were much concerned with love – though in what might be seen as mutually exclusive ways. These were the Troubadours, those wandering singers of songs and tellers of stories, and the Cathars, a break-away group of Christians who were swiftly declared heretical when their teachings became widely known and increasingly popular.

Both were concerned with love, as has been said; and the acts of the Grail are also the acts of love. But to understand how this is so we need to examine the way in which the message contained in the stories grew out of an ancient gnosis, re-interpreted by Medieval man and joined, in his mind, with a triple response towards the teachings of Christianity.

On the one hand, there was *agape*, divine love – of man for God and God for man – represented by the doctrines of the Roman Church and dispensed by the orders of monks: Benedictine, Cistercian, and Franciscan, who interpreted the teachings of the God of Love by means of sermons and commentaries on the Scriptures.

Against this, at the other end of the scale, stood *eros*, profane love – of the flesh rather than the spirit – a dangerous way celebrated by the Troubadours, whose cult became one of the strongest alternatives to the morality of the Church and the piety of its monks, and whose writings, so closely allied to the creation of the first Grail texts, reflect the mingling of Eastern with Western doctrines of love.

Between these two opposing (though not necessarily irreconcilable) points stood the sect known as the Cathars, who harnessed something of each to their own complex beliefs. This lead them to follow a way which taught that the flesh was evil and that only by living a pure and spiritual life could the divine spark of humanity be reconciled with God. To this end they chose to call their priests *perfecti*, 'perfected ones', who followed a way not unlike that of the Grail knights of Muntsalvache in Wolfram's *Parzival*.

Despite appearances to the contrary, these widely differing approaches to love are *not* mutually exclusive, but are linked by the Grail mystery itself, and by the character of Sophia, (Divine Wisdom) on whose role we have already touched.

To begin with the Cathars, it is necessary first of all to correct the popular view of them as life hating fanatics. They were indeed dedicated to reaching the highest possible goal of human achievement – that is, in the spirit – and to this end they saw no alternative but the exclusion of gross matter, concentrating instead on the inner reaches of the soul rather than procreation and the acquiring of worldly goods. In this they were no different from the monks who sought God in the desert, and donned hair shirts to remind themselves constantly of the evils of the body, and lived lives as bereft of comfort as possible. Both were followers of agape and both sought to know God interiorly and to arrive at a point of spiritual union with Him which they believed could only be achieved through abjuring the flesh and living a simple existence. Indeed, the more one reads in the annals of Medieval philosophy the more one is forced to believe that the differences in aim between the orthodox Christian and the Cathar heretic were marginal. They may have differed in the description of the God with whom they sought to be re-united, but they shared a deep-rooted desire to return to a state of innocence and purity from which both believed they had been cast out.

And, they shared another belief – that a part of God had gone willingly into exile with them, and remained there in the person of the figure variously refered to as Sophia, Divine wisdom, or the Shekinah. Beyond this, it is the points of divergence which stand out.

For the Cathars the God of Israel was false, a Demiurge who invaded creation and warped the design of the true God, imbueing matter with a taint of evil from the start. In this they show their origins as basically Gnostic, or as stemming from that subtle blend of gnosis which flourished in the second century AD under the name of Manichaeanism. But as Sir Stephen Runciman points out in his study of *The Medieval Manichee*, [77] 'the origins of Gnosticism remain obscure', though he adds that it is partly to be sought in 'the age-long magical tradition' as well as Hermetic and Egyptian doctrines. Its part in the mysteries of the Grail will become clearer as we proceed.

In essence then, what did these early challengers of orthodoxy believe? It could be said, without excluding anything of major import, that their chief concern lay in the definition of good and evil, their own part in the origin of the world, and the continuing battle for redemption which resulted. Acknowledging the existence of evil, their solution to the problem, as Runciman puts it 'was to take from God the responsibility of having made the visible world' (ibid). Instead they propounded a distant First Cause, God the Father of Light, of whom the Demiurge, the actual creator of our world, was only a fragmentary representation. In this act of false creation, some of the original, primal light became trapped in the bodies of the first men, and thereafter the greatest single objective of the Gnostic (as of the Cathar) was to bring about the freeing of that 'divine spark' and of bringing about its reunion with the true God. In this they had help from Christ, who while he never became man as in orthodox belief, was nevertheless seen as a Son of the True God, sent into the world of matter to aid in its redemption.

So humanity began, almost by accident, with grains of original light trapped within him, each of which must spend itself trying to be reunited with God. Thus the drama of exile, which was to be played out again in the orthodox story of Eden, was firmly founded. In due course, the Grail became a key which lead back to the original, lost state of innocence, a gateway between the worlds of matter and spirit, darkness and pure light.

Thus light and darkness are shown as interpenetrating within the world of space and time, at the nexus of the two worlds (that same nexus which for the orthodox was manifest by Christ's birth in human form, and for the followers of the Grail in the cup itself), and a cosmic struggle began which is seen as continuing throughout time.

In various other Gnostic texts, as well as in many other books of esoteric wisdom, Lucifer, the Prince of Light, is seen as the principle hero of this struggle, fighting, as his name would suggest, to bring light into the darkness of the wrongful creation. In this he becomes a type of Christ and though it may take some effort to accept the fusion of two characters normally opposed to each other, we will find that if we do so the nature of the Gnostic story becomes clearer, and the part played by the Grail in all this takes on a surprisingly central role.

Lucifer, worshipped as a sun god in the Zoroastrian religion, does battle against the legions of darkness. In the words of a modern Gnostic text, which embodies much earlier beliefs,

> With his green wings wide open, transported by his own inner fire, followed by a host of faithful angels, he makes for the centre of the world; his sword of green light, straight in front of him, is in the grip of his powerful hand . . . [2]

At the centre of the world squats the Beast, the embodiment of evil, which Lucifer must destroy. But all he succeeds in achieving is the dislodgement of his adversary, who falls even deeper into matter, while the heroic Lucifer remains trapped in the heart of the visible world. Evil's place is taken by '. . . the most beautiful and ardent and potent of the Angels of the Father, the light bearer, the beautiful Lucifer . . . . He stayed there, where he is now, in the invisible centre of our universe.' (ibid.) But the sword of green fire (green being the colour traditionally associated with Lucifer in all the myths) falls from his grasp.

[It] crossed . . . space and lost its power and light. . . . Obeying the law of concentration . . . it grew denser and denser. At last it became a stone, a wondrous emerald shaped like a cup, and it fell on the surface of the sidereal body. . . because it was pointed it became concave; because it was formed to split, to dissolve, to blast, it became adapted to collect, to unite, to mould; because it was a sword it became a vessel. (ibid.)

Here we see clearly the actions of the Grail. Lucifer's sacrifice is a humane act, made at great cost. This, surely, is the secret hinted at in Wolfram's *Parzival*, where the Grail is a glowing green jewel fallen from heaven or the crown of Lucifer, carried on a green *achmardi*, becoming a talisman for the guardians of the hidden temple.

But there is still another interpretation of this story. A 'Jewel from the crown' can mean more than a stone. It can also be an aspect of personality, a presence of light who in this instance chooses to remain voluntarily in exile in order to transmit a rumour of that light to mankind. In the Biblical story of Eden this is retold anew – when Adam and Eve are driven forth into exile, part of the light of paradise goes with them. In Judaic tradition, as we have seen, this is the Shekinah, Sophia, Wisdom of God, and in Qabala she is called *lapis exulis*, or materialised Shekinah, the shadow bride of God who is called the stone of exile – a much closer approximation of Wolfram's *lapsis exilis* than any of the other possibilities we have so far examined. In a certain sense this figure stands for the mystical heart of the Church, the esoteric strand of Christianity of which the Grail is also a part.

THE 'PERFECT' MEN

Many of these ideas became enshrined in the beliefs of the Cathars, who established a firm foothold in a part of France known as the Languedoc. There, centres of learning, of music, medicine and philosophy (based largely on those of the East, with which trade was well established) flourished. There existed a thriving industry in the translation and study of Arabic manuscripts and Qabalistic learning. Eastern medicine, philosophy, science and alchemy were openly taught and discussed. Carpets, richly inlaid weapons, silks and jewels poured into Europe through these channels.

A period of political, economic and religious flux existed at this time, and the Cathar priests were able to wander far and wide, consolidating their hold over the people of the South and extending their sphere of activity into Italy and parts of Germany and Spain. Word of this began to reach the ears of the Pope, Innocent III; and Bernard of Clairvaux, who was later to have a profound effect on the history of the Grail, harangued the population, claiming that their churches were empty and that they had no true priests. He met with a mixed reception, cheered in some places, booed in others, and soon returned to his monastery.

A new order of monks, lead by the Spaniard Dominic de Guzman (later St Dominic) began tramping the roads in pursuit of the *perfecti*. At first, they attempted to persuade their followers by gentle speech, but soon they began to mount open verbal attacks on the Cathars.

When this failed to have any noticeable effect, stronger measures were sought, and when in 1208 a papal officer named Peter of Castelnau was murdered, at the behest, it was said, of Raymond IV, Count of Toulouse, a known supporter of the heretics, this was all the excuse Pope Innocent needed to raise a crusade against the Cathars. He found the nobility of Northern France only too willing to wage 'holy war' against their neighbours, and the Pope was too concerned to stamp out Catharism to look too closely into the motivation of his allies.

There is no space, and neither is it desirable to chronicle the horrors of the Albigensian Crusade in detail. Others have done so fully[73]. Thousands perished on the swords of the Crusaders, or in the fires laid by Dominic de Guzman – who once addressed a crowd of chained heretics with the words; 'When you heed not the blessing of the Church, you shall heed the stick. We will stir up against you princes and prelates. Towers shall be destroyed and walls broken down, and you shall be reduced to slavery'[51].

It has not yet been possible to prove one way or the other that the Cathars possessed any secret knowledge of the Grail, though there is a strong tradition which suggests that they did. There are however, several points which indicate a very close similarity of intent with the nature of the Grail's message.

Shortly before he was to die in the fires of the Inquisition, a Cathar Bishop named Girard of Montefiore remarked that: 'It is not I alone whom the Holy Spirit visits. I have a large family on earth, and it comprises a great number of men on whom, on certain days, and at certain times, the Spirit gives light'[51]. Such words could have been spoken by the Grail king in almost any of the texts, and could have refered to the family of the Grail, visited indeed by the Holy Spirit 'on certain days and at certain times' – as in Wolfram's poem, where a dove descends to lay a sacred Host on the stone of the Grail.

Certainly the notion that the Cathars in some way possessed inner knowledge of the Grail became a generally accepted fact, as is shown in an incident which took place during the final siege of Montségur, the great Cathar citadel in the Pyranees, which held out longest of all against the invading armies of the North.

Montségur, whose name so closely resembles Muntsalvache, the name of the Grail mountain in Wolfram's poem and the *Titurel* of Alberecht von Scharfenburg[74], was ruled over by the Countess Esclamonde of Foix, perhaps the most famous of the many women *perfecti*. Indeed, so revered was she, that many refused to believe in her death, shortly before the destruction of Montségur, believing her to be sleeping until doomsday in the caves which riddled the mountainside beneath the castle. Many besides identified her with the Grail maiden Repanse de Schoye.

It was in these circumstances that the incident mentioned above took place. During the final long siege of Montségur, a member of the family of Esclamonde, the flamboyant Roger of Mirepoix, dressed himself in white armour and appeared on the walls of the citadel with a golden-hilted sword held on high. At this sight many of the besieging army fled in terror, believing that the Knight of the Grail himself had come against them.

Another story, probably apocryphal, describes how the original Cup of the Last Supper was hidden in the cave of San Juan de la Pena in 713 (though it is not suggested how it came there) by an Aragonese Bishop named Audebert. When Aragon was threatened by the Moors at the beginning of the twelfth century, the sacred Cup was removed and taken to the Pyranees, where it was entrusted to the Cathars. When they were destroyed, the Cup was smuggled back into Spain and hidden in the cave again, this time under the protection of Don Martin L'Humain, the then King of Aragon. In later years the Cup was identified with one kept in the Cathedral of Valencia, but which had now further acquired the identification with the vessel given to Solomon by the Queen of Sheba. Wildly improbable though this story may seem at first glance there is a ring of authenticity about it. Nor should one overlook the fact that it is to the Cathars that the precious object is entrusted.

In due course, Montségur fell; its defenders were killed or burned, without trial, below the walls. To this day the place has an atmosphere of horror to which many bear witness. If this was the home of the Grail, it has retained none of its sanctity. However, the story is told that on the night before it fell, four of the *perfecti* escaped over the walls and thence into the mountains, taking with them their Holy Books and other secret treasures, among which was believed to be numbered a certain cup.

Whether or not they bore the Grail is not important for the purposes of our argument. If some of the *perfecti* escaped, as seems more than reasonable, they took with them the secrets of their faith. For every hundred heretics who perished, half as many again escaped into the mountains and beyond, into Italy and Germany, where their treasures were probably scattered.

But their doctrines and beliefs lived on, and their continuance can be traced through widespread traditions of esoteric knowledge, according to which some of those Holy Books found their way into the hands of Rosicrucian adepts, carrying the knowledge of the Cathar Church, the *Eglise d'Amour*, or Church of Love, as it was called by them, into the centuries which followed[35].

Into the Grail texts themselves, elements of Cathar belief filtered widely. In Chrétien de Troyes '*Lancelot*'[13]. One of the foremost works embodying the new ethic of Courtly Love, the Knights of King Arthur, after communion, give each other the kiss of peace, according to the custom of the Eastern Rite, and which the Cathars took over in their rite of the *manisola*, the Love Feast, which itself suggests both the imagery of the Last Supper and the banquet of the Holy Grail.

The Cathars, for all their belief in the evil nature of the flesh, their desire to transcend their humanity and to find oneness with the true God of Light, were true adepts of love – not the profane sensual love celebrated by the Troubadours – but a spiritual *agape* which differed hardly at all from that of the orthodox Christians. They were filled with a burning anguish of spirit, which drove them to the greatest possible endurance (in fact the Cathar rite, called the *endura*, involved many hours of fasting – sometimes to the point of death – in which they purified themselves to become vessels of light). This they did out of love of God, the Light; and it *this*, rather than any possible truth in their having possessed the Grail, which makes them one with its universal brotherhood.

The Cathars understood perhaps better than any the message of the Grail of Love, which above all involves service and dedication to the Light. They carried with them always the one Gospel in which they found expressed a true knowledge of that Light – the Gospel of John. Therein they read the Divine Mandate that God was Love, and that to be with Him was to dwell in love.

THE SINGERS OF LOVE

All this was understood by the Troubadour poets also, though in a very different manner. Their way was through the adoring of the Feminine Principles, one of whose names is also Sophia, and there is evidence too that the troubadours were by no means ignorant of Cathar beliefs. Their operation in the same area of France alone makes this more than likely; but there is besides, much more evidence, much of which has been collected by Denis de Rougemont in his famous study *Passion and Society*[21].

De Rougemont has, for example, pointed out that one of the first, as well as foremost, of the troubadours, Pierre Vidal, wrote a song in praise of hospitality, which though on the surface looks innocent enough, becomes less so when it is known that all the castles and hospices mentioned were either actual Cathar strongholds or were situated in areas where they were particularly active.

De Rougemont goes on to list some of the other similarities between Cathar and troubadour ways of life, that they:

> ... extolled (without always practising) the virtue of chastity; that, like the Pure, they received from their lady but a single kiss of initiation; that they distinguished two stages in the *domnie*, [service to ones lady]... as the Church of Love distinguished between Believers and Perfect. They reviled the clergy and the clergy's allies, the members of the feudal caste, They liked best to lead the wandering life of the Pure, who set off along the road in pairs[21].

The one problem which does seem to preclude any close identification between Catharism and the Troubadour ethic — the hatred of physical love of the one against its celebration by the other — vanishes when one accepts that the Troubadours celebrated not actual, physical love at all, but rather an abstract, distanced worship of womankind, even of the Divine Feminine itself. Troubadour songs abound in sentiments which exhibit this symbolic attitude, with Love as an imperious Queen, reigning over her subjects with Goddess-like power. She is at once an earthly sovereign, and, by extension, every woman addressed by the practitioners of Courtly Love. At the same time, she also represented Mary, the Heavenly Queen, behind whom stood Eve, the first woman, and Sophia, the semi-divine symbol of Wisdom.

Courtly Love, as well as possessing an actual court, with all the rules and etiquette which were part of this, was also seen as a semi-religious order, a true *eglise d'amour*, with its own laws and rules for worship.

Thus, a man might look at a woman, might woo her, desire her, and might vocalise that desire in endless panegyric – but he was expressly forbidden to do more. Actual physical congress was never permitted – at least, not by those who obeyed the Rule of Love, as set out in tracts such as *The Art of Courtly Love* by Andreas Capellanus[21], which may accurately be described as the Troubadour's bible.

Nor were the ideas expressed in Andreas' book new. In the East, as early as 1022, the Arabic poet Ibn Hazm had written his *Tawq al-Hamana* (The Dove's Neck-Ring) in which he spoke of a chaste love which was a sign of the highest natural attainment of a noble man. Andreas, as well as the greater body of his contemporaries, took up this idea, and others like it, and embroidered them into a Western Courtly system designed for the seeker after love. The Provencal word *jois*, which has no precise rendering in English, but can be said to mean something like 'blissful joy', was coined specifically to describe the object of the quest – the whole purpose, means and end of which are summed up in one tremendous line, written by the thirteenth century Troubadour Uc de St Circ:[1] 'To be in love is to stretch toward heaven through a woman.' Whether we choose to see this woman as Mary, Sophia, or simply as the Eternal Feminine, we must believe in the force with which such statements are made.

From this point it is not difficult to see that what binds the Troubadours and the Cathars together in an underlying unity of spirit, is their feeling for the 'femininity' of God. The singers and poets of Provence, exposed to the words of the wandering perfecti, worshipped at the throne of the Divine Feminine, whether addressed as Lady Venus, Mary or Sophia, the Shekinah of the world. The Perfecti, abdjuring *eros*, sought the underlying principle of *agape*, personified again as Sophia, the sacred vessel of knowledge, a figure inherited from Gnosticism.

The Gnostics themselves had encountered at some point the influence of Eastern thought in the form of Sufi doctrines. Here again the theme of chaste love was found, turning towards a search for *spiritual agape*. From this tremendous mingling, or as Denis De Rougemont puts it, 'the final confluence of the "heresies" of the spirit and those of desire . . .[21] arose the Courtly ethic, which in turn gave rise to the impulse of the Grail narratives, both known and unknown. From this we can see that there is a natural debt of succession devolving from the Gnostics to the Troubadours and Cathars, finally emerging in the matter of the Grail which binds all these threads together in the vast monolith of the Arthurian epic cycles – the natural outcome of a hunger for original truth, face-to-face contact with the Deity, and a longing to return to the first home, Eden or Paradise or Heaven.

EXERCISE 3: THE GREEN STONE

Close your eyes and imagine you are standing before a great round church capped by a magnificent dome. Above this rises a great golden crescent which catches the sun and gives back its light with powerful radiance. The walls are ornately carved with intricate patterns, and two vast doors stand open to admit you into the cool depths beyond.

Within, all is dimly lit and echoing. As your eyes grow accustomed to the light, you see that the building is truly of mighty proportions, the soaring dome seeming to stretch up to heaven itself, while the walls are lined with colonnades of pillars ornately carved. From four small openings in the roof, beams of sunlight filter down, illuminating a point towards the centre of the building. You are drawn to go forward to that spot, and notice for the first time that the floor is of beaten earth, with none of the magnificent tessellated flooring you might have expected in such a place.

At the centre, where the four beams of light meet, is a rough, conical mound, in which is a low, narrow opening large enough to admit one person at a time. Peering in, you see a small chamber, lit with torches. You enter and find yourself in a room with bare, earthen walls, in the centre of which is a low altar. On this is set a great faceted jewel, an emerald more bright than anything you have ever seen before. In its thousand surfaces you catch glimpses of many things; your own image, and other images that seem to move and turn within the heart of the stone. In one you see the figure of a wounded man, lying upon a bed, in another a knight kneels with a shining cup in his hands. Another facet shows you three mailed riders pursuing a brilliant star. Yet another holds a perfect rose, which emits light . . . .

For a long time you watch spellbound as the light of the torches plays across the surfaces of the Green Stone, showing you many things. But at last your trance is broken by a movement in the chamber. Two men have entered, one clad in chain mail with a white cloak on which is emblazoned a red cross; the other, clad in a plain robe of white, carries a leather-bound book. These two take up their places at either end of the altar, and facing towards each other begin a chant which rises and falls in measured cadences, filling the room with sound. The words seem to be in Latin, with some that may be old French, but you seem able to understand them despite this . . .
(PAUSE.)

The sound and the meaning of the words fill your mind, and you feel at peace with the world and with your life as you have perhaps not done for a long time. You are given the grace to forgive yourself whatever faults you may feel you have committed; whatever hurt or sorrow lies within you is slowly dissolved. In the presence of the Green Stone and its guardians you feel only joy and an overflowing sense of well-being which transcends all the outward shape of your life . . .

At length the song finishes. In the silence of the chamber you hear a sigh which you know is the sound of all fears, doubts, and uncertainties being expelled from you and from the place of the Stone. Light hearted, you emerge from the chamber like one new-born and walk through the great dim church to the doors. Outside, all is brilliant sunlight, and you go forth into the world renewed and strengthened . . .

Slowly bring yourself back to the place in which you began this meditation. Its memory will remain with you for many days to come, and you will find that merely recalling the song and the joy you felt then will continue to irradiate your whole being with light.

PART TWO:
INITIATIONS

4 · THE FAMILY
OF THE GRAIL:
GUARDIANS AND GODS

THE HOLY BLOOD

Those who go in search of the Grail are following the impulse of their spiritual blood. The description of the Grail in certain texts as *San Greal* (Holy Grail) in others appears as *Sang Real* (Holy Blood), the changing of a single letter describing a wholly different concept. The idea of the existence of a Grail 'Family', chosen to act as guardians of the sacred vessel, seems to arise from this, and in the works of Robert de Borron and the Vulgate *Queste*[55], Joseph of Arimathea does indeed establish a line of Grail Kings who, in their turn, have to keep the Grail securely and administer its secrets to each one of their successors. These secrets have been inviolably guarded throughout the ages, each Grail author commenting obscurely upon them, or else refusing tacitly to discuss them. Wolfram von Eschenbach's theory is expounded by the hermit Trevrizent, who after a long disquisition on the meaning of the Grail itself, tells Parzifal the true nature of the Grail Family: 'Maidens are given away from the Grail openly, men in secret, in order to have progeny . . . in the hope that these children will return to serve the Grail and swell the ranks of its company'[92].

Wolfram here speaks of a fleshly succession, but he also indicates that the dispersion of the Grail lineage is a secret known only to the angels. Earlier in the text he had spoken of the troop of angels who

71

had left the Grail on the earth to ensure that 'A Christian progeny bred to pure life had the duty of keeping it. Those humans who are summoned to the Grail are ever worthy.' (ibid.)

Robert de Borron, in his *Joseph d'Arimathea*[64] gives an account of the company who sailed from the Holy Land under Joseph's leadership, experiencing many adventures along the way. Here the Grail Family is presented in a fully rounded form. Joseph receives the message of the Grail directly from Christ, who visits him in the tower where he has been imprisoned after the disappearance of the Saviour's body: 'he spoke to [Joseph] holy words that are sweet and gracious and full of pity, and rightly are they called Secrets of the Grail.' (Trans. by Margaret Schlauch *Medieval Narrative* Gordian Press, 1969.) Thereafter Joseph is kept alive by the power of the Grail, which provides him with food just as it later provides materials for his ancestor Titurel to build the Temple of the Grail.

Released from prison by the emperor Vespasian, Joseph is instructed by the voice of Christ. He sets up a new Table in imitation of the one at which the Last Supper and the first Eucharist was celebrated. One place represents the place of Christ, another, which is to remain empty until the rightful Grail knight appears, stands for that of Judas. When Joseph's followers are seated there they 'perceived a sweetness which was the completion of the desire of their hearts.' (ibid.)

For a time the company of the Grail remain somewhere in Europe until a desire comes upon them to divide their number. One Petrus, named, we may safely assume, after the disciple Peter, sets off for 'Avaron', a land to the West which can only be the Celtic Otherworld of Avalon, or perhaps Glastonbury in Somerset, where legends of Joseph's coming and the Grail still abound.

Another of the Grail lineage, Bron, whose name so closely echoes that of the Celtic God Bran the Blessed, and who becomes known as the Rich Fisher after he feeds the company from a single fish in emulation of Christ's feeding of the 5000, becomes Joseph's successor and the new guardian of the sacred vessel. Joseph is bidden by the Voice of the Holy Spirit to relinquish the Grail into the keeping of Bron, who will take it to a safe place and there await the coming of his grandson, Perceval.

> And when that son arrives, the Vessel shall be given over to him, and do thou tell him and command him to charge him with its keeping thereafter. Then shall be accomplished and revealed the significance of the blessed Trinity which we have devised in three

parts . . . . And when thou hast done this thou shalt depart from this world and enter into perfect joy which is My lot and the portion of all good men in life everlasting. Thou and the heirs of thy race . . . shall be saved . . . and shall be most loved and cherished, most honoured and feared of good folk and the people. (Trans. Margaret Schlauch, ibid.)

So Joseph does as he is bidden, assembling the whole company and relaying to them all that the voice has instructed him to do, '. . . saving only the word that Christ spoke to him in the dungeon. This word he taught to the Rich Fisher, and when he had said these things he also gave them to him written down.' (ibid.)

THE GRAIL TEMPLE

Thus the Secrets of the Grail are passed on, from father to son, until the time came for the Quest for the Grail to begin in earnest. Until then it was kept in a safe and secret place, a temple where it could be reverenced until such time as mankind was deemed ready to be told of its existence, shown its miraculous powers, and offered the chance to go in search of what it represented.

From the start certain features appeared fixed. The temple usually stood at the top of a mountain, surrounded by either impenetrable forest or a stretch of wild water. Access, if any, was more often than not by way of a narrow bridge (though other variants are possible), and this bridge often had a sharp edge, from which it became known as the Sword Bridge. Sometimes, to make the entrance even harder, the Temple would revolve rapidly, so that it was necessary to judge the moment exactly before leaping for the single entrance as it flashed by.

One of the most detailed pictures of the Grail Temple appears in a thirteenth century poem called *The Younger Titurel*[74], composed around 1270 by a poet named Albrecht von Scharfenburg. He drew widely on Wolfram's *Parzifal* and devoted altogether 112 lines of his work to a description so specific in detail that it seems more like an actual description than poetic fancy.

The story runs thus: Titurel, who is the grandfather of the famous Grail knight, Parzival, was 50 when an angel appeared to him and announced that the rest of his life was to be dedicated to serving the Grail. He was then lead into a wild forest from which arose a mountain called the Mountain of Salvation, or Muntsalvach. There he found workers recruited from all over the world who were to help him to build a castle and temple to house the Grail, which at that time floated in the air over the mountain, held there by angelic hands. So

Titurel set to work and levelled the top of the mountain, which he found to be made from solid onyx, and which, when polished 'shone like the moon'. Soon after, he found the ground plan of the building mysteriously engraved on this fabulous surface. It was to take thirty years to build, but during this time the Grail provided not only the substances from which the temple was built, but also food for the workmen. At length it was complete, and it is at this point that we find the following description, which is worth quoting in full:

The Temple arose as a wide and high rotunda, bearing a great cupola. Twenty-two chapels stood out in octagonal form; over every pair of chaples stood an octagonal bell-tower, six storeys high. At the summit of each tower was a ruby surmounted by a cross of white crystal, to which a golden eagle was affixed decorated by many goldsmiths. At its summit was a carbuncle, which shone forth at night. Should any Templar return late to the castle, its glow showed him the way . . .

Two doors lead into each of the chapels. Each one contained an altar of sapphire, which was so placed that the priest should face to the east. The altars were richly decorated with pictures and statues; over each one a high ciborium. Curtains of green satin protected them from dust . . . . In the east stood the main chapel, twice as large as the others. It was dedicated to the Holy Spirit, who was the patron of the temple. The chapels to either side of it were dedicated to the Holy Virgin and St John.

On the wall between the chapels were golden trees with green foliage, their branches filled with birds. Golden-green vines hung down over the seats; roses, lilies and flowers of all colours could be seen . . . . Over the vines were angels, which seemed to have been brought from paradise. Whenever a breeze arose they came into movement like living beings.

The portals were richly decorated in pure gold and in every kind of precious stone which was used in building . . . The windows were of beryl and crystal, and decorated with many precious stones, among them: sapphire, emerald, three shades of amethyst, topaz, garnet, white sardonyx and jasper in seventeen colours . . .

The cupola rested on brazen pillars, into which many images were graven. It was decked with blue sapphire, on which stars of carbuncle shone forth both day and night. The golden sun and silver-white moon were pictured there . . . cymbals of gold announced the seven times of day. Statues of the four Evangelists were cast in pure gold, their wings spread out high and wide. An emerald formed the keystone of the cupola. On it a lamb was depicted, bearing the cross on a red banner.

In the midst of the temple was a rich work dedicated to God and the Grail. It was identical in form to the temple as a whole except that the chapels were without altars. In this the Grail was to be kept for all time. (Trans. J.& D. Meeks.)[24]

Here the magical vessel was kept, watched over by a select body of knights drawn from the Family of the Grail. Wolfram called them *Templiesen*, Templars, and while it is possible that he meant simply 'guardians of the temple' by this term, few would doubt that he is making a more than casual identification of the Grail knights with an actual body of men, whose history, like that of the Cathars discussed in Chapter 3, was tragic and wrapped in mystery.

THE WARRIORS OF GOD

In 1118 a Burgundian knight named Hugh de Payens, together with eight companions, all Crusaders, founded a new order of chivalry, dedicated to poverty, chastity and obedience and established specifically 'in honour of Our Lady' and to guard the pilgrim routes to the Holy Land. This was something wholly new in the Western world, though similar orders existed in the East. The idea of combining the piety of a monastic way of life with the rules of Chivalry must have seemed as startling as it was original. Yet little is known about the man who founded the order except that he described himself as 'a poor knight', and held a small fief at Payens, only a few miles from Troyes, where Chrétien wrote the first Grail story some sixty-two years later.

The other significant fact about Hughes de Payens is that he was related to Bernard of Clairvaux, one of the most famous theologians of the age and the founder of the Cistercian order. It was to Bernard that Hughes now wrote, begging him to sponsor the new order and to give them a Rule by which to orient their lives.

After some hesitation Bernard took up their cause, and it was largely due to his influence that the order was ratified at the Council of Troyes in 1128. They were permitted to wear a white robe with a red cross emblazoned on the right shoulder, and were given, as their headquarters in the East, the building believed to have been the Temple of Solomon in Jerusalem. From this they received the name by which they were ever after known – the Knights Templar.

From this beginning grew the single most famed military organisation of the Middle Ages. The Templars became the permanent 'police' of the tiny war-torn kingdom of Jerusalem, They fought with utter dedication and became feared by Moslem and Christian alike. St. Bernard's Rule was a harsh one, binding the knights to forswear home and country, to fight at need to the death for the holy places of Christendom. For the sake of chastity they had to sleep fully clothed in lighted dormitories; nor were they permitted to receive private letters – any communication had to be read out aloud before the company. They must attend mass at least three times a week wherever they were, accept every combat that came their way, despite the odds, and neither ask nor give quarter.

Despite this, Bernard's sponsorship alone was sufficient to swell the ranks at a rapid rate. Soon the order began to build a network of castles, called 'commanderies', across the Holy Land, as well as in France and England and elsewhere in Europe. Their power and strength increased, and their wealth grew accordingly. Though each individual forswore personal possessions, they gave freely of their goods to the order, and began also to win much treasure in their battles with the Moors. In time they became so wealthy and of such good standing that they virtually became the bankers of Europe, lending huge sums to help finance the Crusades. And, as their political power grew, so their enemies increased. Finally, the miserly and avaricious King of France, Philip the Fair, plotted with a renegade Templar to bring about their downfall – for the most astonishing of declared reasons.

Philip charged the Order with heresy, and in a single night had the greater part of their number taken prisoner. They were tortured, and under pressure admitted to every kind of crime, from sodomy to spitting on the Cross. The last Grand Master of the Knight's Templar, the saintly Jacques de Molay, was executed on 19 May 1314, bringing the order effectively to an end one hundred and ninety-six years after its foundation.

Such are the historical facts. Behind them lies an even more remarkable story, one which is closely linked to the inner history of the Grail.

There are several facts about the Templars which bear notice. Firstly there is their name, which though it is said to derive from the Temple of Solomon is also reminiscent of the *Templiesen* of Wolfram. Then there is the connection with Bernard of Clairvaux. As well as the Rule he wrote at the request of Hughes de Payans (to whom he dedicated it) *A Treatise on the New Knighthood*[5] in which he speaks of the Order in terms which are easily applied to the Grail knights. He wrote:

It seems that a new knighthood has recently appeared on earth, and precisely in that part of it which the Orient from on high visited in the flesh. . . . It ceaselessly wages a twofold war both against flesh and blood and against the spiritual army of evil in the heavens.

The idea was something wholly new. Though the Church had long seen itself as the army of God, this had never been taken to the extreme of actually arming its priests. The idea seemed mutually exclusive. Yet this is precisely what the Templars became, priests and soldiers 'doubly armed' writes Bernard, so that they 'need fear neither demons nor men'. Adding that 'these are the picked troops of God', and exhorting them that

precious in the eyes of the Lord is the death of the holy ones, whether they die in battle or in bed, but death in battle is more precious as it is the more glorious. . . . If he [the knight] fights for a good reason, the issue of this fight can never be evil. (ibid.)

Yet these men, who as Bernard says will be 'in company of perfect men' (how reminiscent of the Cathar perfecti), are later reviled, their order discredited and destroyed. Why should this be so?

Among the list of crimes, both sacred and secular, of which the Templars were accused, are listed the harbouring of the Cathars and of friendship to the Islamic sect of the Ismaelites – their nearest equivalent in the East. Both accusations are possibly true, at least in part. The order did offer sanctuary to wrongdoers, provided they forswore their former lives and obeyed the Templar rule. The period of testing was lengthy however, and discipline strict. It is also more than likely that certain of the Cathars, fleeing from the South, did find their way into the Order, and may even have influenced it from within. At any rate it is interesting to note that the Templars were widely known to accept men with a past, and that records exist which suggest a curious form of absolution for such men. It is said to have taken the form of the following words: 'I pray God that He will pardon you your sins as he pardoned them to Saint Mary Magdalene and the thief who was put on the Cross'[51].

The Templar who vouchsafed this, Galcerand de Teus, under torture was persuaded to admit that the 'thief' referred to here was to be understood as Christ (rather than one of the thieves traditionally supposed to have been crucified alongside Jesus). He added that at the moment the Lance of Longinus pierced the side of the doomed Messiah he 'Repented that he had said he was God the King of the

Jews, and having in this way repented concerning his sin, he asked pardon of the true God and thus the true God spared him . . .' (ibid.)

This remarkable 'confession' is startlingly like the stated beliefs of the Cathars, as well as harking back to earlier Gnostic teachings. It is significant also that it places the incident at the moment of the piercing of Christ's side with the Lance, which was later identified as the Grail spear. While to the Inquisition it offered a further instance of Templar heresy, it also may be seen as a link between the Order and the Cathar movement.

As to the suggestion that the Templars were friendly with the Islamic sect of the Ismaelites, this is also likely enough. Though the order began with the avowed intention of destroying the infidel and of winning back the Holy Sepulchre permanently for the Church, constant encounters with the Arab way of life had a transformative effect on the relations between East and West.

THE HEAD IN THE DISH

It has been suggested that the Templars may also have been the guardians of a relic of such importance that it even outshone the Grail – though in fact the two were connected. According to the argument put forward by Ian Wilson[91] and more recently by Noel Currer-Briggs[17] both of whom offer considerable documentation, there is every reason to believe that the object known as the Mandylion passed through the hands of the Order during the height of its power, and that this same object, which seems to have been a piece of cloth, folded several times and stretched between frames of wood, may have been the shroud of Christ, apparently lost to the world during the siege of Constantinople in 1204, but possibly disguised in this form to prevent it falling into Moslem hands. It is this same relic which is nowadays to be found in the Cathedral of Turin, and is the subject of continuing controversy and world-wide scientific investigation.

If Wilson and Briggs are right, and there is no reason why they should not be, then not only does this present the Templars as possessing a sacred relic, it also goes some way towards explaining another of the 'blasphemies' of which they were accused.

This concerned the worship of a graven idle called Baphomet (usually accepted as a corruption of Muhammad) and described as a bearded head wearing a crown. This could easily be a garbled understanding of the Mandylion, which was folded so that only the bearded face of Christ, marked with the wounds caused by the Crown of Thorns, appears.

In both the *Perlesvaus*[6] and the Cistercian-inspired *Queste del Saint Graal*[56], which was part of the Vulgate Cycle composed at St Bernard's monastery at Clairvaux, there are echoes of this mysterious image. In *Perlesvaus* King Arthur himself witnesses the Grail mass, and when he looks towards the altar: 'It seemed to him that holy hermit [who was officiating] held between his hands a man bleeding from his side and in his palms and in his feet, and crowned with thorns. . . .'[6] While in the *Queste* we find Galahad at Mass in the Temple of Sarras, the Holy City of the Grail, where the vessel is kept in an Ark standing upon a silver table – an image that reflects both the Temple of Solomon, and also the model of the Holy Sepulchre found in every Templar commanderie throughout the world, where their most sacred rites were performed.

So we have the Templars, based at the site of Solomon's Temple, guarding a sacred relic, holding a special devotion to the Virgin, supported by St Bernard – elements all recognisable from the Traditions of the Grail. Approved by the Pope, their rule written by one of the foremost churchmen in the Western world, they became for a time the highest standard of earthly power. The whole of Western Christendom had grown used to the idea of the knight. The Templars were super-knights, combining the skill of fighting men with the spiritual fervour of the priesthood. We should not be surprised if many of the Grail writers took the Order as a model not only for the Grail chivalry, but also for the Round Table.

And here too the notion that too much power carries its own built in law of self-destruction is apparent. Might can be harnessed for right; but when there are too many wrongs to right, when the Kingdom of Jerusalem had been secured, however uneasily, the Templars, like the Round Table, fell apart. Accumulations of wealth and power served only to provoke jealousy and fear. The earthly Jerusalem was only a symbol of the heavenly city after all – discontent bred of by heaviness of time and stale custom shook the high purpose with which the Crusaders had set forth. In consolidating an earthly kingdom they had lost sight of the heavenly one. A scapegoat was required, and the Templars provided it.

And so, by a supreme irony, the Warriors of God, whose order had been founded to uphold the highest ideals of Christendom, as well as of knighthood; which had been blessed by the foremost churchmen of the time, were themselves accused of the very same evils which had only recently been levelled at the Cathars – the denial of God, the defamation of the Cross, the worship of false idols, and the practice of unnatural vices.

79

So close, indeed, are the accusations, that one is almost led to believe that behind the garbled confessions, extracted by torture, confessions of things only half understood (by both sides), lies a body of teaching which would make the Templars the truer inheritors of the Cathar heresy, their aims and beliefs the same, yet perverted and twisted by the change from passive to active roles in the world.

THE CAUSE OF LOVE

Perhaps we may look to the part played by St Bernard for further illumination. Just as, within the disciplines of love, there were three approaches, so outside this area there were three ways: that of love itself, that of knowledge and wisdom, and thirdly, the way of action. It was to this third way that the order of the Knights Templar dedicated themselves, becoming first and foremost, despite their innate spiritual trend, a military order. From Monks of Love they became Monks of War, and in some senses at least Bernard of Clairvaux was responsible for this.

It is easy to see why, as more than one commentator has observed, Bernard came to see his own order, the Cistercians, as a superior force in the struggle against the heretics in the South. Several of his sermons are given over to a bitter attack on the Cathars of Germany, whom he had never even visited. With the advent of the Templars, he saw the strength of this Christian force as directed 'against a spiritual army of evil in the heavens'. Perhaps he was trying to reconcile love and war, by embracing both.

Henry Corbin, the great authority on Eastern and Western religions, made the point in his book *The Fight for the World-Soul* (1952), that there is a battle for the soul of the world going on continuously, and that St Bernard was aware of this and tried to defuse the situation from both sides by harnessing love and war together. His chief agents in this would have been the Templars, and it is perhaps this as much as anything which hastened their demise. In fighting against the heresy of Catharism they were fighting their own inner impulse.

There was always an inner court within the order, consisting of the Grand Master and eight others – a tradition which sprang from the original founder and his companions. If there were any secret activities, beliefs or practices within the Order, these men would have been directly responsible for it. They would almost certainly remain silent even under torture, and the jumbled fragments which were extracted from the lesser members of the order would be no more than half understood pieces of a much larger whole. It is unlikely that we shall ever know the truth. What does seem certain is that the Templars are the most likely candidates for the transmission of the Grail message from the Cathars to the mysteries of Alchemy and the parables of the Rosicrucian adepts.

THE HIDDEN KINGS

The Temple of the Grail, wherever it stood, whether in the realm of fancy or of fact, was established in the minds and hearts of the Medieval Grail seekers. Whoever its true guardians may have been, they continued to carry out their appointed task – as they surely continue to do today. Of those whose names rise to the surface from the mists which surround the inner Tradition of the Grail, certain figures stand out. We might name Melchizadek, the priest king of Salem, who in Biblical tradition made the first offering of bread and wine long before the Eucharist was celebrated in the Upper Room in Jerusalem. Solomon himself, master of Wisdom, seems to have held the Cup, or at least the symbolic powers it contains, for a time, and to have passed it on to others of his line. Even Jesus, who prayed that the cup of his agony might pass from him, may be in some senses a Grail guardian. While Joseph of Arimathea, and the line he founded, carried the mystery into the age of Arthur and beyond. Perceval's part-coloured half-brother Feirefiz, wedded to the Grail princess Repanse de Schuoy, begot of her a son who was named Lohengrin, and he in turn sired an even greater figure of mystery and might.

The first mention of this character, little more than a rumour, comes in a medieval chronicle which for the year 1145, relates how a certain Bishop Hugh of Cabalah visited Rome and was told how, some years previous to this,

> ... a certain Priest and King named John, who lives on the further side of Persia and Armenia, in the remote East, and who with all his people were Christians ... had overcome the royal brothers *Samiardi*, Kings of the Medes and Persians, and had captured Eckbattana, their capitol and residence.... The said John advanced to the help of the Church of Jerusalem; but when he had reached the river [Tygris] he had not been able to take his army across the river in any vessel. He had then turned North, where he had learned that it was all frozen by the winter cold. He had lingered there for some time, waiting for the frost, but because of the wild weather ... [was] forced to return home after losing much of his army because of the unaccustomed climate[79].

With a touch of colour the chronicler adds that Prester John is 'said to be of the lineage of the Magi who are mentioned in the Gospel, and to rule over the same people as they did, enjoying such glory and prosperity that he is said to use only a sceptre of emerald. . .' (ibid.) We are reminded by this of the emerald Grail – this is not surprising when we consider its bearer's lineage.

But what was the truth behind this extraordinary account? We have to remember that at the time the threat of invasion from the East hung over the West rather like that of Atomic war in the twentieth century. The perilously slender hold of the Crusaders over the Kingdom of Jerusalem was constantly in danger of failing, with a consequent inrush of Muslim armies expected to follow. News of a crushing defeat 'in the furthest East' was a morale booster comparable to hearing that Hitler's forces had been turned back by the Russians during the last war. Thus we must admit at once that there is a strong element of wish-fulfilment behind the various references to a 'Christian king in the East'.

Be that as it may, in 1165 there appeared a mysterious letter, copies of which found their way to Pope Alexander III, the King of France, the Emperor of Constantinople (Manuel Commenius), and the Holy Roman Emperor Frederick I – the spiritual and temporal rulers of Western Christendom. The letter purported to come from no lesser person than Prester John himself, and it is a most intriguing document.

The letter begins:

Prester John, by the Grace of God most powerful king over all Christian kings, greetings to the Emperor of Rome and the King of France, our friends. We wish you to learn about us, our position, the government of our land, our people and our beasts. . . . We attest and inform you by our letter, sealed with our seal, of the condition and character of our land and men. And if you desire. . .to come hither to our country, we shall make you on account of your good reputation our successors and we shall grant you vast lands, manors, and mansions[79].

The letter continues in this style for some twenty pages, describing a land overflowing with goodness and riches, ruled over by the benign Priest King, whose crown is the 'highest. . .on earth', and whose sway extends over forty-two other Christian kings. The writer then goes on: 'Between us and the Saracens there flows a river called Ydonis which comes from the terrestrial paradise and is full of precious stones ... and of each we know its name and its magical power.' (ibid.) The letter ends by exhorting the rulers of Christendom to put to death 'those treacherous Templars and pagans' and is signed 'in the year five hundred and seven since our birth'.

The letter is a forgery, of this there can be no doubt. The style, as well as the contents, clearly derive from identifiable sources – mostly Eastern – an ironic fact when we consider that Prester John was set up as a bitter foe of the Muslims! What we do have in the text of the letter is a description of the Otherworld, a semi-attainable, paradisial place filled with wonders, offering spiritual as well as temporal pleasures. Rather like the country of the Grail in fact, as much of the text bears out. Indeed, we should hardly be surprised to find the extraordinary Temple of the Grail from Alberecht von Scharfenburg's poem to appear in this setting. Both are the product of the same impulse, the desire to return to our home, the Earthly paradise from which Adam and Eve were driven forth.

Prester John, as here presented, is a recognisable archetype, belonging to the race known as 'Withdrawn Kings', once great and noble beings who have withdrawn to an inner plane of existence, from where they watch over the progress of humanity and occasionally take a direct hand in historical events. Merlin is another, as are Melchizadek, the Biblical Enoch, King Arthur, and the angelic Sandalphon. John, whose title means simply 'Priest-King' is the product of several vague historical personages, half remembered accounts of Alexander the Great, various kings of Ethiopia and more than one Tartar lord.

But he is something more than this. Whether Wolfram found a reference to Prester John as the offspring of the Grail knights, or whether he made up the connection, he touched upon a deep nerve. John represented all that was best in Christendom. He suffered none of the traits of corruption or heresy which hung over much of the West like a dark cloud. He was all powerful, all good, and he was the guardian of a great secret – the Holy Grail.

THE WORK OF THE GRAIL FAMILY

The descent of the Grail lineage is thus a metaphysical one. It includes mystics, seekers after truth, alchemists, magicians, Kings, and many more. Whatever its provenance, it remains a symbol of man's desire for union with God, the return from exile on earth to a home in Paradise.

Lancelot at the Chapel of the Grail by Evelyn Paul

Certain individuals are assigned to this task of restoration – some with a specific duty and goal in mind – others who have no clue as to their errand but who together share in the Family of the Grail. They make up what we might term the Tribe of the Grail, a tribe drawn from no earthly lineage, with no specific racial descent; a tribe which has no territorial boundaries, no common basis for belief other than the symbol which reunites all opposites – the Grail itself.

As one of the greatest modern commentators on the Grail Tradition, Walter Johannes Stein, wrote, as long ago as 1928:

The Grail race has the mission of expanding to cosmopolitan proportions all that belongs to the narrow group, of enlarging separate interests to world interest. In our time this mission lies no longer with the family group. How the present day faces the impulse will only become clear as through our consideration of the ensuing centuries, we step by step draw nearer the problem[80].

THE TABLES OF THE GRAIL

We have seen how Joseph of Arimathea set up a Table which became a symbolic expression of the Table of the Last Supper, having twelve places plus one, and one which remained empty in token of the betrayer Judas – a place which would only be filled when the chosen Grail knight arrived who could sit in the Perilous Seat without danger.

This was the second Table of the Grail. The Round Table, made by Merlin 'in the likeness of the world' was the third. Together they make up a triple emanation of the Holy Spirit which is the central Gnosis of the Grail. Each succeeding emanation is further from the point of origin, but containing the essence of the rest.

Thus, all who sit at the Table of the Grail inherit the fullness of the earlier Tables, for there has come into being a fourth table, where all who are engaged upon the great Quest find themselves led inevitably in the end. Some set out with no specific task in mind, like Perceval; others feel they are acting on the impulse of the Divine Will, as Galahad does. And there are those who become lost in the webs of a labyrinth of conflicting interests who never arrive at the place intended for them – those who seek an earthly city, a physical relic, and who will never achieve the Grail until they understand that not by deeds of arms, nor feats of endurance, will they gain their heart's desire. Instead they must seek a subtler form of alchemy which unites human and divine.

There are those who may discover their Grail in a nearby place, where they had not thought of looking; the rejected stone the *lapis exillas*, is transmuted into the sacramental stuff of life by a simple act of love, or of devotion. The transformations taking place at the altar of Divine Love is every bit as valid as the transmutations of the psyche achieved by magical means.

In the end, all become part of the Grail Family. They meet in the circular Temple so reminiscent of Templar churches and chapels. And they discuss the actions of the Grail in the world: how its operations work towards the healing of the planet, and of the great divide in the human psyche which lead to the dualism of the Gnostics and the Cathars. In so doing they learn. The lessons of all who go in search of the divine are taught to them and they either listen to or ignore them. Finally, they are caught up, transmuted, changed out of all recognition; they become one with the divine impulse and walk in the great places of the Spirit which have so many names:

Eden, Paradise, Avalon, Shambhala. In time they may be sent out again, openly or in secret, to spread the word of the Grail to the rest of humanity.

This is the work of the Family and it is not always easy. Opposition, as we saw in Chapter 4, will almost certainly be encountered along the way. That this may be overcome, or itself transmuted, is one of the gifts of the Grail which are available to all who seek it out. In the end it becomes more than a symbol, more than an idea; becomes instead a life giving force which permeates the whole universe, until it glows with the fire of divine love and light.

EXERCISE 5: JOINING THE FAMILY OF THE GRAIL

We have already seen something of the importance of the direct links between the Grail guardians of each age. In the two-part pathworking which follows you are led into the world of two such guardians: Prester John and Sophia Aeternitas. These two represent the masculine and feminine elements of the Grail tradition, and once contact with them is established the work of the seeker will be much enhanced. The two parts of the meditation should preferably be done on succeeding days, or at least with no more than a week separating them, but preferably not on the same day. The gifts and knowledge imparted will become increasingly important as you progress on the path of the Grail.

PART ONE

As you begin to relax, breathing slowly and evenly, the room in which you are sitting slowly fades, and you find that you are standing in the open air, high up on top of a range of hills, with a view of much of Britain spread out below you. A little to your left is a low mound, not unlike the old Prehistoric burial mounds, and in it is a heavy wooden door let into the side at the Eastern end. You approach the door, and as you do so it opens before you. All is dark at first within, but as you enter you become aware of a soft glow which lights your way. Inside, the mound seems much larger than it did from outside, and you see that a tunnel opens out from it, sloping away into the earth. It is lined with very ancient looking blocks of stone which look as though they have always been there.

As you follow the path downwards the slope grows steeper, though never too much to walk comfortably along it, and the gentle light remains steady and unchanging. In a while you come to another door, much like the one by which you entered, and this too swings open to the touch. You pass through and find yourself in a hall of vast proportions. You can only dimly see the roof far above, and the walls on either side recede into darkness. The floor of the hall is paved with huge blocks of masonry, fitted so exactly together that they are perfectly smooth and even to walk upon.

As you proceed across the floor of the great hall you become aware that the light ahead of you is brightening, and you begin to see where two great thrones stand, carved out of rock and decorated with the likeness of strange beasts. Seated in the left hand throne is the figure of a man who appears to be deeply asleep. He is tall, regal and bearded, and wears a crown of three tiers, surmounted by a dome. His robes are of deepest blue, with elaborate letters in silver embroidered on them. These seem to move and change subtly as you look. In his arms the figure holds cradled a sceptre carved out of emerald, on top of which is set a silver rose.

In the second throne is a figure who appears at first much like the first, so that they might be brothers. He also wears a crown, this time with four tiers with a great cross surmounting it. He is robed in scarlet with designs in gold which seem like stars and suns, always moving in an endless dance. He carries a sceptre carved from red jasper, tipped with a cross of gold.

In front of the two thrones is a low table made from a single block of marble, and on it stands a small bronze bell suspended from a dark wooden frame. Hanging from the frame is a striker, and you understand that you must go forward and strike the bell once, but no more. (PAUSE.)

With the first sound of the bell, which echoes softly in the huge hall, the figure on the left stirs, though he does not yet open his eyes. But now the bell continues to reverberate, even though you have laid down the striker, and with the second reverberation the figure on the right also begins to stir. Thereafter, with each echo of the bell the two become progressively more awake, until at last they are fully conscious and gaze smiling down upon you.

Now you become aware that while you were engaged in your task with the bell, the hall behind you has filled up with a multitude of people. People who are dressed in the fashions of many ages, from the furthest days of the Neolithic and Bronze Ages, to the most recent times. They are of every race, colour and creed, Indians, Arabs, Chinese, Slavs, all these and many more. Some appear careworn and sad, others afraid, but all have a look of dawning certainty and assurance as they stand before the two figures in their great stone chairs.

As you look at the two we have awoken, they seem to grow blurred to your eyes, and slowly they merge with each other. As your sight clears, you see that there is now only one figure on the left hand throne, and that his crown is of seven tiers, domed and surmounted with a cross of gold and emerald. His robes are now of purple, with patterns of sun, moon and stars, and letters inscribed of gold and silver upon them. The sceptre he bears is of emerald, tipped with a golden cross in the centre of which is a silver rose.

As you stare in awe at this mighty figure, a great cry comes from the crowd which now seems to fill the hall. They are calling out many names in many tongues, but you hear only one. It is PRESTER JOHN, the name by which the figure is known to you from the writings of the wise in your own land.

Now he beckons you to approach, and when you stand before him offers you a gift, either in the form of a message or an object of some kind. Remember what is said or given to you. (PAUSE.)

After a time you find that you are again standing before the throne of Prester John with the great crowd, who now begin to come forward to speak with the Priest King in turn. Many days will pass before all have spoken with him, and many more will enter the hall who may yet know nothing of this place. But for you the time has come to depart. Salute the figure in the throne and then turn away and retrace your steps across the great hall, through the tunnel and outside again onto the hillside overlooking most of Britain. Slowly let the images of earth and sky fade until you find yourself once more where you began. The memory of what you have learned will remain fresh in your mind and may lead you to further explorations into the inner realms.

PART TWO

As your senses adjust to the state of meditation visualise yourself as standing on the deck of a ship which is already at sea. A strong wind fills the sails and the ship moves swiftly through the water. In the distance ahead you see a line of tall cliffs which grow gradually closer until you are able to see the details of lichen and birds nests along the cliff edges. The ship enters a narrow channel between dark rocks and soon you arrive in a sheltered inlet which forms a natural harbour. The craft docks against a jetty constructed of massive blocks of stone, and stepping ashore you walk inland through deep woodland filled with the noise of streams that trickle down to the sea on every side.

Emerging from the wood you find yourself in a narrow valley at the head of which a waterfall plunges down from the cliffs far above into a deep pool. On either side of the waterfall are two giant stone chairs like the thrones of ancient kings, and standing between them are two angelic figures, the one on the right dressed in green, the one on the left in red. They are the guardians of the valley and all that lies within.

To the right of the waterfall is a narrow crack in the face of the cliff, wide enough at the bottom to admit one person at a time. The angel in red indicates that you should enter, and this you do. Within is a dimly lit passage, and it is only a short distance to a pair of doors of ancient dark wood, which open at a touch, admitting you into a vast hall, the walls of which lead off to right and left, vanishing in shadow, and the roof of which is too far distant to see. A gentle light allows us to see where we are. The floor is made up of huge stone blocks, set smoothly together so that the cracks hardly show.

As we proceed the light grows stronger and you begin to see glimpses of mighty stalagmites hanging from the roof, each one pulsing with its own inner radiance. Then ahead you see two great stone chairs, their backs towards you. They are smaller than the vast carvings you saw outside at the feet of the mountains, but of the same kind. As you pass the chairs and come round to the front you realise, with something of a shock, that this is the same hall you have visited before, in which you first met the great figure of Prester John. Once again you see him seated in majesty, in his purple robe emblazoned with sun, moons and stars, and bearing a sceptre carved from a single emerald.

The throne next to him is now occupied by the figure of a woman, dressed in a robe of red. She is veiled and carries a white sceptre tipped with a carved red rose. Upon her robe are embroidered the letters S A. Both the figures seem lost in meditation, sitting unmoving with indrawn sight.

In front of the two thrones is a cubic altar, upon which is set a golden stone, emitting sufficient radiance to touch all who stand before it. You should respond to this as you wish, letting it sink deeply within you as you stand in silence before the King and Queen.

As before you become aware of a bell in a wooden frame, which stands upon the altar beside the golden stone. This time however the bell is of silver, and as you lift the striker and touch its side to the bell a sweet ringing tone is emitted which continues to reverberate through the vast hall. At its first sound the two figures stir, looking down upon us from the two great thrones. They indicate that you should approach, choosing whether you will stand before the mighty figure of Prester John, or before the veiled Lady whose initials are S. A. They will have a message or an instruction which you should remember . . .

When you are returned to your place you become aware that, as before, the hall is now filled with a great multitude from every race and time that have filled the world. But, where before their faces seemed care-worn or fearful, now they are filled with radiance and joy. Turning again to the great King and Queen you see that they have risen from their thrones, and together with the multitude you bow your head for a moment in homage.

Looking up again you see the mighty archetypal figures hold out their hands in blessing above the throng; then together they descend and, hand in hand walk slowly from the hall, vanishing at last behind a curtain which hangs to one side of the thrones. In the silence which follows their departure the great multitude of people from all ages begins to disperse, vanishing silently back into the shadows of the great hall. A small group remains about the altar however, and these now invite you to take hands with them in a circle. You do so and all begin to dance slowly around the golden stone. As if in answer its light grows brighter, filling your ears and heart and mind with a golden glow . . .

At last this begins to fade, and with it the shape of the hall and the people with whom you danced fades also. You awaken to find yourself back where you began this journey.

5 · WASTE LAND AND WOUNDED KING:
HEALING WITH THE GRAIL

GRAIL KINGS AND ANTI KINGS

There is an ancient (and admittedly dualistic) saying that all things have their opposites. Thus just as there is a Grail, and Grail Kings, and Grail Knights, so there is a black Grail, anti-Grail Kings and evil knights who seek the ruin of the kingdom of the Grail.

These things are seldom spoken of, or written about, in our time, though the medieval writers knew of their importance. But they remain a necessary part of the mystery, providing a balance to the darker side of the myths. At the nexus point, in the heart of the Grail, is a point of harmony, of resolution, of polarity, which is brought about through the *interaction* of the darkness and light which surrounds the Grail.

To avoid the darker side of these stories is to close our eyes to a very real problem. There is a great deal of casual-seeming cruelty in the Quest texts – the casual slaying by Gawain of pagans in a city which had become Christianised is one such example, though it would have seemed perfectly normal and proper to a medieval audience; or the episode where Bors is about to go to the rescue of a woman in distress when he sees his brother Lional, tied naked to a horse and beaten with a thorn twig by an evil knight who is carrying him into captivity. Bors has to make a choice between brotherly love and his knightly vows, and being the staunch Quester that he is he opts for the latter. But the woman he rescues is herself a demon in disguise, and although his brother is rescued by Lancelot, when the brothers next meet there is such anger on the part of Lional that they almost kill each other.

The Quest by William Ernest Chapman

This kind of situation is common throughout the Quest, and we are likely to encounter the same kind of thing on our own journey – not literally the same of course, but no less difficult or painful because of that. What we must never expect is that the Quest will be easy, or that we will become miraculously sorted out people before we begin. Many, if not all the Grail mysteries are about self discovery, hence the emphasis on questions. The Quest is a journey inward as well as through the lands of the Grail.

For this reason it is useful to know about some of the adversaries the Quest knights encountered, so that we can recognise their like if, and when, they crop up.

THE DOLOROUS BLOW AND THE MAIDENS OF THE WELLS

Two themes which appear continually in the texts relating to the Grail are the Wounded King and the Waste Land. These are inextricably linked because the former is generally the cause of the latter. There are several stories which deal with this in detail, but for the moment we will look at just two of them. In Malory's *Morte d'Arthur* we find the following description of what is known as 'The Dolorous Blow'.

Balin le Sauvage is following the track of an otherworldly woman, and along the way he finds himself in the company of a friendly knight. But this man is murdered by an unseen foe, and Balin soon learns that he is called Garlon, and that he rides under a cloak of invisibility. Balin arrives at the castle of King Pellam of Listenesse, who is about to hold a great tournament, and there he discovers Garlon, who is pointed out to him as 'he with the black face; he is the marvellest knight that is now living, for he destroyeth many good knights, for he goeth invisible'. Observing Balin watching him, Garlon strikes him in the face and in a moment of fury Balin takes out his sword and strikes him dead. 'Anon all the knights arose from the table to set on Balin, and King Pellam rose up fiercely, and said, "Knight, thou hast slain my brother, thou shalt die therefore or thou depart."' In the fight that follows Balin's sword breaks,

> 'And when Balin was weaponless he ran into a chamber for to seek some weapon, and so from chamber to chamber, and no weapon he could find, and always King Pellam after him. And at last he entered a chamber that was marvellously well dight and richly, and a bed arrayed with cloth of gold, the richest that might be thought, and one lying therein, and thereby stood a table of clean gold with four pillars of silver that bare up the table, and upon the table stood a marvellous spear strangely wrought. And when Balin saw that spear, he gat it in his hand and turned him to King Pellam, and smote him passingly sore with that spear, that King Pellam fell down in a swoon, and therewith the castle walls brake and fell to the earth, and Balin fell down so that he might not stir foot or hand. And so the most part of the castle, that was fallen down because of that dolorous stroke, lay upon Pellam and Balin three days.' (Bk XVI. Ch.15.)[52]

The spear is the lance of Longinus, with which he had struck a blow into the side of Christ on the Cross. Used thus to defend and wound, rather than to protect and heal, it causes a hurt that cannot be healed until the coming of the Grail knight.

Before we look at the second example, we should notice two things about this version. Firstly there is the way in which the blow comes to be struck – not just through Balin's impetuous actions, but ultimately because of Garlon, the Invisible Knight. Secondly that the effect is local rather than general. It is the Fisher King Pellam's lands which are laid waste rather than the whole kingdom of Arthurian Britain.

93

The second text is called the *Elucidation*[22]. It was intended as a kind of prelude and explanation to Chrétien's *Conte Del Graal*, although in fact it does very little to make things any clearer, not at first sight anyway. The beginning of the story goes like this:

'Now listen to me, all ye my friends, and ye shall hear me set forth the story that shall be right sweet to hearken unto. . .[of] how and for what cause was destroyed the rich country of Logres whereof was much talk in days of yore.

The Kingdom turned to loss, the land was dead and desert in suchwise as that it was scarce worth a couple of hazel-nuts. For they lost the voices of the wells and the damsels that were therein. For no less thing was the service they rendered than this, that scarce any wandered by the way. . . but that as for drink and victual he would go so far out of his way as to find one of the wells, and then nought could he ask for fair victual . . . but that he should have it all. . . .The damsels with one accord served fair and joyously all wayfarers by the roads that came to the wells for victual.

King Amangons, that was evil and craven hearted, was the first to break the custom, for thereafter did many others the same according to the ensample they took of the king whose duty it was to protect the damsels and to maintain and guard them within his peace. One of the damsels did he enforce, and to her sore sorrow did away her maidenhead, and carried off from her the cup of gold that he took along with him, and afterward did make him every day be served thereof. . .thenceforth never did the damsel serve any more nor issue forth of that well for no man that might come thither to ask for victual.' (ibid.)

Afterwards, we are told, was the kingdom laid waste 'that thenceforth was no tree leafy. The meadows and flowers were dried up and the waters were shrunken, nor as then might no man find the Court of the Rich Fisherman. . . .' The Damsels of the Wells, in whom we may see a memory of a female priesthood who guarded the mystery of the Grail and its healing springs, serve no more. The land is dried up, and cannot be restored until the coming of the Grail knight, who in other texts is called 'He Who Frees the Waters'.

Here we have a quite different version of the events which caused the Waste Land, but once again it is the actions of an anti-Grail character, Amangons, that is the direct cause.

There is evidence to show that the names Amangons and Garlon derive from a single etymological source, and that a third name,

Klingsor (or Clinschor), applied to the black magician in Wolfram von Eschenbach's *Parzival*, also derives from this same source.

If we look for a moment at this third figure we will begin to see more. Klingsor is described as a mighty sorcerer of the line of Virgil (in the Middle Ages the famous Roman poet had achieved the reputation of a magician), who rules over Castle Mortal or the Castle of Wonders, an evil fortress which stands in opposition to the Castle of the Grail. Dark stories are told of him.

> There was a king of Sicily called Ibert, and the same of his wife was Iblis . . . Clinschor became her Servitor till she rewarded him with her love. . . .The King found Clinschor with his wife, he was asleep in her embrace. If his was a warm bed he had to leave a deposit for it – he was levelled off between the legs by royal hands. . . .The King trimmed him in his body to such effect that he is unserviceable to any woman today for her sport. Many people have had to suffer as a result[92].

Here Klingsor's evil is partly attributed to his emasculation, for which he takes revenge on all who come within his sphere of power. A darker tradition indicates that he practised self-castration in a magical operation which gave him a terrible strength. He is thus seen as diametrically opposed to the Maimed King whose wound, also a sexual one, is caused by the hand of another.

By looking at these three texts we arrive at a kind of composite portrait of an Anti-Grail King, a dark aspect of the actual guardian. In the case of Garlon, he is described as Pelles' brother, and there is a suggestion that the same relationship once existed between Klingsor and Anfortas, the Grail King in *Parzival*. Amangons, though not related to Arthur by blood, functions as a kind of opposing force before the coming of Mordred later in the stories.

Each of these characters is then, in some sense responsible for the advent of the Waste Land, which, from a purely localised event, becomes more widespread and generally felt in the later Arthurian texts. So that by the time we get to the thirteenth century story of *Perlesvaus*, the failure at the heart of the Arthurian kingdom, which is illustrated by the Waste Land, has become more directly linked with the actions of Arthur himself, whose failure to take the initiative in the Quest – leaving it to his knights instead – is to be seen as a failure of will and the empowerment of his sovereignty.

In this sense the Waste Land has become indicative of a more general malaise – the heart of the Kingdom, its King, is ailing, and until both are healed, by the finding of the Grail, the sickness will not be cured.

This is an important theme which runs throughout all the Arthurian tales, and in those which deal with the Grail is particularly central. Throughout the earlier part of his career Arthur plays an active role – fighting battles, getting the sword Excalibur from the Lady of the Lake, setting up the Round Table. At one point, he even experiences the mystery of the Grail directly, though he does not seem to do anything about it, and already there are indications of a certain malaise. The passage in question is found in *Perlesvaus*, and contains one of the most vital clues to the inner meaning of the Grail.

Now, the story tells us that at that time there was no chalice in the land of King Arthur. The Grail appeared at the consecration [of the Mass] in five forms, but they should not be revealed, for the secrets of the sacrament none should tell save he whom God has granted grace. But King Arthur saw all the transubstantiations, and last appeared the chalice; the hermit who was conducting the mass found a memorandum upon the consecration cloth, and the letters declared that God wanted his body to be sacrificed in such a vessel in rembrance of Him. The story does not say that it was the only chalice anywhere, but in all of Britain and the neighbouring cities and kingdoms there was none[6].

After this Arthur almost disappears from the scene, the attention of the stories moves to the Quest and we hear scarcely any further mention of him except as a titular figure-head. Only with the end of the Grail quest and the gradual decline of the Arthurian court which ends with the breaking of the Round Table Fellowship, does Arthur move back to the centre of the stage. It is almost as though he falls asleep for the duration of the Quest, waiting like some enchanted being for the magical word or talisman that will awaken him.

And this, of course, is exactly what happens. Although it is never spelled out in any of the texts, Arthur is himself a wounded king – Pelles, Anfortas, Titurel are only surrogates who bear the wounds of the King as their own.

We get a hint of this again in *Perlesvaus*, where Arthur has actually gone on an adventure of his own, and meets with a chastening experience. Taking part in a tournament, he wins a golden crown and a war horse. But the knight who offers him the prizes does not recognise him. He says:

Sire, you have won in combat this golden crown and this war-horse, for which you should rejoice indeed, so long as you are valiant enough to defend the land of the finest lady on earth, who is now dead. It will be a great honour for you if you have strength enough to protect that land, for it is great and rich and powerful indeed.

'To Whom did the land belong?' asked the king, 'And what was the name of the queen whose crown I see.'

'Sire, the king's name was Arthur, and he was the finest in the world, but many people say that he is dead; and the crown belonged to Queen Guinevere, who is now dead and buried, which is a grievous pity[6].

Arthur is not really dead, but the sickness which afflicts all the land had affected its people too, so that they believe the king has deserted them.

Another text, *The Didot Perceval*, attributed to Robert de Borron[78], makes it even clearer. Merlin prophecises, in words that seem to apply to Arthur as much as to the Grail King, that:

The...king has fallen into a great sickness and into great infirmity, and know that [he ...] will never be cured ... until a knight foremost those who are seated at this table has done mighty deeds of arms, of bounty, of nobility ... and when he will have asked what one does and whom one serves with the Grail, the...king will be cured ... and the enchantments will fall which at present are in the land of Britain[78].

Arthur does not *seem* to be physically wounded it is true, but if one remembers his connection with Bran the Blessed, discussed in Chapter 1, and who does possess such a wound, then the identification is further strengthened.

The point is, indeed, that Arthur *has* to be the Wounded King. Nothing else will satisfy the need to explain the Waste Land, which though it is only a part of his kingdom, extends symbolically over the whole of the land.

If we then list the points as they appear from a reading of the texts we find that:

1. Arthur had once played a more central role in the Quest for the Grail, leading, as we saw in Chapter 1, a raid on the Otherworld to bring back the proto Grail.

2. In the later stories his role has become passive or inactive, and that he remains at home awaiting the return of the knights from the Quest.

3. In the older, Celtic stories, the figure of Bran the Blessed occupied a position similar in many respects to that held by Arthur *and* the Wounded King, and who was also held in a state of suspended life awaiting a ritual act that would free him.

For though the Entertainment of the Noble Head is seen as having a negative outcome – the return of the Company and the burial of the Head at White Mount – there is another way to see this; as the inevitable working out of a series of events which culminates in the installation of Bran as Guardian of the Land.

Arthur, as we saw, later dug up the head, thereby assuming the mantle of that guardianship himself. If we need any further evidence we have only to look at Arthur's own end as Malory describes it in the *Morte d'Arthur*:

> More of the death of King Arthur could I never find, but that ladies brought him to his burials; and some such one was buried there [in Glastonbury] that the hermit bare witness to . . . but the hermit knew not in certain that he was verily the body of King Arthur . . . . Yet some men say in many parts of England that King Arthur is not dead, but had by the will of our lord Jesu into another place; and that he shall come again. . . . I will not say it shall be so, but rather will I say, here in this world he changed his life. But many men say that there is written upon his tomb this verse:

> HIC JACET ARTHURUS REX,
QUONDAM REXQUE FUTURUS.
> (Book XXI. Ch.7.)[52]

In this 'other place' Arthur was to remain, perhaps in perpetual sleep, until such time as his country needed him again – at which time he would come forth in splendour, accompanied by all the panoply of Faery, to defend the Land.

In other words Arthur, like Bran before him, was a Sacred King, a guardian of the land itself to which he was so closely connected that he could not even leave it, even in death. And in this he was not only like Bran, but like the Wounded King also. In fact, he was the Grail king, to all intents and purposes. This was why he remained in Camelot awaiting the news that would signal the end to his own torment. The inner realm of Britain, which in all the stories is called Logres, was also the Waste Land of the Grail texts. Even its name, which is a corruption of the French word *orgueilleuse*, proud, makes sense in this context. Logres, Arthur's kingdom, is the Proud land indeed, and suffers because of it.

The medieval writers never bothered to set this down because to their audiences the mystery was no mystery at all – they knew Arthur was the Wounded King and that the wound was, like the food of the Grail, of the spirit. And because of it the whole land lay under enchantment, it was wounded by the wounding of its Lord, and awaited his healing so that it, too might be healed.

HEALING OURSELVES

In the same way, we have to cure our own inner ailments; our divided selves must be reunited just as, to speak for a moment in Gnostic terms, the innate goodness of the human soul desires to be reunited with its higher self – God. Not for nothing is Perceval refered to as 'the Good Knight' – like the Gnostically-inspired Cathars who called themselves *parfaits*, good men, and who carried their part of the Grail mystery into the heart of Medieval Europe, (see Chapter 3). He is a distillation of the human condition. His tests and trials, his agonies, are ours, to a greater or lesser degree according to the depths of our involvement in the Quest.

Above all else the Grail Knights strive to reconcile the opposing forces which surround the object of their search. The Grail is a symbol of unity and reconciliation, and as such it requires that we lay to rest the ghosts of our own inner malaise. As one writer puts it:

Imagine yourselves always in your spirit, as pure, deep, luminous vessels, open to the cosmos, standing on the earth but firmly closed against the outer world. The cosmic and divine streams flow into your cups and make the divine spark within them luminous and glowing. This luminosity then penetrates outside and streams as blessings upon all life. It is a wonderful ceaseless giving and taking, an eternal circulation which must never be disturbed by your own damaging thoughts, because only if your heart is pure all this can take place for the blessing of all life[70].

If the Waste Land is to be healed and the Courts of Joy, which are its opposite and cure, are to be built we must each find a way to heal the wounds we ourselves bear. As the same writer just quoted puts it:

Your thoughts and feelings, whether good or bad, the earth on which you live absorbs and digests. You provide her nourishment – if you love the earth and think kindly and divinely the earth is health and radiates. If you do not love her, and have dark and destructive thoughts, she becomes sick and dark, and one day her wounds break open. (ibid.)

Thus is the Waste Land caused, by our neglect and our 'dark and destructive thoughts', which are externalised in the form of characters like Amangons, Garlon and Klingsor.

As we said at the beginning of this chapter, as there is a Grail of light so there is a black Grail. This is a statement which requires qualification. The Grail is the Grail is the Grail and can be nothing else – but there are always those who would misuse its power, which is neutral rather like the power of the neutral angels who, according to Wolfran von Eschenbach, first brought the Grail to earth. And here again we see the paradox: the Angel of Light falls, is renamed Satan, the Devil; yet from his crown comes a fragment of the original, pure light he at one time emitted.

The Grail is thus as much within the keeping of the anti kings as it is in that of the Grail Family – Joseph of Arimathea and his kin. It is in our care also, and we must learn to use its power wisely.

All of which is just another way of saying that the Quest is unlikely to be easy and demands a level of service that is of the highest kind. But, once that initial commitment is made, once the first steps – however halting – are taken on the road through 'the Grailless Lands', then *already* the rewards are prepared. It is up to us, finally, whether we overcome the negative aspects of the Quest within ourselves, the anti Grail kings and their servants, and have in the end the satisfaction of seeing the dual aspects of the search united in one – the ultimate mystery of the Grail.

THE TIMES ADVENTUROUS

Although the enchantments, the magic and the phantasmagoria of the Times Adventurous in which the knights of Arthur sought the holy vessel are on another plane to that where we live today, there is no lack of continuity between the two worlds, which overlap at all times and in all places eternally. As a recent Grail seeker has unforgettably put it:

> [throughout] these untoward adventures, told in all sincerity, there pierces a higher truth. Historic verity obtains in the descriptions of warring creatures, in the clash of monk with initiate, of priest with pagan, of devotee with druid. In the forests, on wild wastes, by hills and vales for ever unexplored, this subtle conflict rages unceasingly. It is not otherwise in the Quest of the Holy Grail, whose battleground is our own soul [or our own world], that 'realm of Logres' whose frontiers no man can define. Blessed indeed is he who has seen the Grail or felt the Divine Presence in outer vision and inner consciousness; his feet are already on the Way. The Times Adventurous await him[76].

As, indeed, they await all the members of the Family of the Grail who follow the thousand and one paths through the forest, across hill and dale and mountain, river and sea, as Tennyson put it: 'following the Gleam'.

EXERCISE 4: THE FIVE CHANGES

The five changes through which the Grail passes, constitute, as we have seen, one of the most mysterious aspects of the Grail Tradition. In the following meditation the energies represented by four of the five aspects are gathered together and channelled through the fifth into the heart of the earth and from there to the seven great continents which form the greater part of the planet. This is a healing ritual of great power and efficacy if performed with the right degree of intent.

To begin imagine that you are standing on the Northernmost pole of the planet. This is not the magnetic pole, but the pole of the earth's axis, around which it spins. Above your head, therefore, be aware of the constellation of Polaris, with the great beacon of the Pole Star at its heart, and around it the constellations of the Great and Little Bears and the coiling form of the Dragon, Draco.

Here, there is no real horizon, no cardinal points to the compass, so that references to East, South, West and North are relative, referring to the true points from which influences pour in from the distant constellations.

With eyes still closed, stand up and face the East. You are looking across the vast sea of space, lit by a million stars. Amongst them you are able to pick out the silver shape of the Bull, the constellation of Taurus. At its centre, like an eye, is the star Aldebaron, a smoky red point of energy sometimes called The Eye of God.

Within this starry form you gradually become aware of another shape, that of a great circular Dish, which catches the light of the stars and reflects it towards us. This light surrounds you and is drawn into your heart centre, where it is gathered up and projected downwards, through the centre of your body, through your feet, and on down in the earth beneath.

From there it branches out towards the points of the Equator, and then inward towards the core of the planet. There, in the very centre of the earth, you see a great crystal Cup, shaped so that it catches light both from above and below and is able also to emit light in either direction.

Now it catches the light you send, the concentrated force of the great Dish, which is that in which you make an offering of all your intentions, and sends it raying out in all directions, striking upwards through the earth until it reaches each of the seven Continents: North America, Asia, Europe, Africa, Australasia the Arctic and Antarctic. Each of these becomes ringed by a line of brilliant light, which remains glowing as you make a 90° turn to the right . . .

You are now facing true South, and ahead across the depths of space you see the constellation of the Lion, whose heart is the bright star Regulus, also known as the Little King. As you look you see that sitting astride the back of the Lion is the bright shape of a radiant child. This is the Divine Youth who will grow to carry the light for all men into the world. Now he raises both hands and throws a long shaft of light across the gulf which separates him from you. Once again it is gathered into your heart centre and from there channelled down into the planet, raying forth beneath our feet to the Equator and then inward to the receptive Cup of the Grail. From there it rays out on all sides, striking upwards into the land masses of the seven continents, islanding them in a second band of light.

Now make another 90° turn towards the West where, across the depths of space, you see the constellation of the Scorpion, a creature sacred to the Goddess Isis. There, you see another dark red star, known as Antares. And, in the midst of the Scorpion, a glowing cube of light, each face of which represents one of the elements of which Creation is formed. As it turns, it rays out a great beam of light towards you, and you catch it and gather it into your heart centre, from where it flows through and down into the body of the planet which is still called by us 'Mother Earth'. There, as before, it reaches the points of the Equator on either side and is channelled inward to the great crystal Cup at the centre of the world. Caught up and sent forth again, it passes upwards until it reaches each of the seven continents, surrounding them in a third band of light, which glows ever brighter.

Turning once more 90° to the right, you now face true North, where you find the constellation of Piscis Australis, the great Cosmic Fish, in whose mouth glows the bright star Formahalt. Below the outline of the fish is the shape of a great Spear, the weapon which, in the story of the Grail was used to wound, but which now sends forth healing light towards you. You capture and distil it forth again from your heart centre, through your feet and into the earth, where the crystal Grail, the final shape it assumes in the the mystery of the Five Changes, waits to catch, and then send forth again, the light you perceive as passing through the earth and then outwards again to each of the seven great continents, building a fourth barrier of light around them.

For a moment hold these images as clearly as you can: see the outlines of the continents islanded in light, and know that this will bring harmony and peace to all who live there, and that the light binds all into a singly unified whole which is the earth. In this way the healing power of the Grail in each of its five forms, is given back to the world a thousandfold, and you also, as a channel for its light, gain benefit from it.

Slowly now, as you watch, the light begins to fade from your sight – though it will continue to shine out in the inner world and do its work for the healing of the planet . . .

Become gradually aware again of your surroundings and awaken gently from the work of the meditation.

6 · THE LIVING HALLOWS:
KNIGHTHOOD FOR TODAY

A TIMELESS MYSTERY

What makes the Grail such an enduring symbol for the inner search is its continuing value for each and every age which has followed upon its first appearance in the world. Men and women have been seeking to plumb the mystery ever since, with varying degrees of success. We have seen something of the outer as well as the inner course which the stories have taken; now it is time to look in more detail at the reality of the experience which the Quest entails, first through the adventures of the original Quest Knights, and then through some contemporary accounts.

The Hallows of the Grail are living symbols of a very real Quest, in which many men and women are at present involved. This new knighthood is every whit as true and valid to the original precepts of chivalry, honour and the search for meaning as were the knights of the Round Table.

THE THREE WHO ACHIEVED

By the time of the *Vulgate Cycle*[56], the many stories relating to the Quest had been synthesised into a more detailed and specific set of allegories. This natural winnowing process left five major characters: three who were successful (though in a qualified way), and two who

The Hallows by William Ernest Chapman

failed (though spectacularly). The three successful questers were Galahad, son of Lancelot and the Grail Princess; Perceval, the 'oldest' of the three in terms of the Tradition; and Bors, who perhaps possesses the most human qualities. The pair termed unsuccessful are Lancelot and Gawain. The best way in which to arrive at the impact felt by the individual seeker for the Grail is to examine the roles of each of these five in turn.

GALAHAD

Galahad is a direct descendent, through his mother's family, of Joseph of Arimathea. He is, from the start, destined to achieve what no other knight of the Round Table could – to take the Grail in his hands to the Holy City of Sarras, and there to receive from the hands of the Grail's True Master the food of divine sustenance – at which point he dies, in what used to be termed 'an odour of sanctity', from the sweet aroma supposed to issue from the dead bodies of holy Saints. He had accomplished the work he was born to do and there was no longer any reason for him to remain.

But what are Galahad's special qualities, and how can an understanding of them help the modern seeker? First of all it is important to understand that Galahad is very much a product of the Middle Ages, of the cult of Saints, and of the deeply mystical approach to religion which typifies the age. Once this is properly understood much that appears strange or inhuman in the character of Galahad becomes surprisingly ordinary. Like Bors, he shows a single-minded determination for the task he has been bred for. No physical attack can overcome him, no temptation of the flesh beset him. It seems as though he could have walked straight into the Castle of the Grail without opposition and finished the Quest there and then. But, as has already been suggested, Galahad is seen as an aspect of Christ, and in this he shares a function of teaching by example – whether it consists of a buffet from the flat of a sword or an act of piety and Christian chivalry.

Thus he must accomplish the mysteries of the Quest as Christ accomplished those of his ministry. He is a clear case of someone who believes implicitly in their own destiny – as very few do today – and partly for this reason his path is the hardest to follow. Yet here is also a living embodiment of Divine Love (Agape) in operation: his perfection, as great as any earthly man can be expected to attain, is born out of a love for all of Creation. He needs to cure the wounds of the Fisher King and the Waste Land before he can enter into the higher mysteries of the Grail.

Galahad is, when all is said and done, little more than a cipher. As the Arthurian scholar Jean Frappier noted, he is 'the culmination of the desire to fuse Chivalry with Religion'[47]. His path is as clear as it could be: his coming, attended by signs and portents, his acquiring of arms, first sword and then shield of a special kind; his adventures, in which he proves himself the superior, both physically and spiritually, of his peers – all these mark him out as the destined Grail winner. Yet when he has done, when the great acts of affirmation, of healing and restoration have been accomplished, there is nothing left for him to do but die – his quest is crowned by this personal apotheosis which, though many might aspire to emulate it, few would actually meet with such whole hearted acceptance.

Thus, when he has partaken of the last mysteries, he takes leave of his companions: 'therewith he knelt down before the table of the Grail and made his prayers, and then suddenly his soul departed to Christ, and a great multitude of angels bore his soul up to heaven, that his two fellows might see it . . .' (Malory, Bk XVII. Ch. 23.)

Not many would attempt this route to the Grail; but lest we dismiss Galahad as a proto Saint, let us remember that his last thought is to ask his companions to 'remember me to my father Sir Lancelot and as soon as you see him bid him remember this unstable world', a message from which we might also benefit if we take the time to understand it. For Galahad the world is more than a cloak of flesh soon to be put off. It is a beautiful and rare place through which he moves with grace and honesty and as much love as he can muster. It is a place worth dying for. But he is his father's son also, direct and powerful and to the point in all that he does. Behind the facade of this pious knight stands a very human figure, from whom, if we wish, we can learn much.

PERCEVAL

Perceval, of course, was brought up in the depths of the forest, in ignorance of such creatures as knights, or concepts such as chivalry. But this was one of the characteristics which enabled the young hero to come so near the centre of the mystery, so much so that he becomes a future Guardian of the Grail. The other particular feature was his simplicity – some would say his foolishness – which earned him the title of the 'Perfect Fool'. This innocence of the world and of worldly matters makes him impervious to the kind of temptations undergone by both Galahad and Bors – to him women are like flowers, brightly coloured creatures designed by nature to care for his needs and make him laugh. He has, in fact, something of the primal innocence of our first father, Adam.

His battles with other knights have a dreamlike quality, as though such pursuits are of little importance to him – as is perhaps the case. Indeed, like both his companions, he has a single minded approach to the Quest which cuts across the various trials set before him almost as though they were not there. It is as though Perceval lived always a little bit in the otherworld.

This same absent-minded innocence gives rise to such incidents as the 'blood in the snow' episode told by Chrétien de Troyes[15]. Here Perceval becomes fascinated by the red blood and black feathers of a bird which has made a kill in the snow. To the young hero they are a reminder of his lady's colouring, her red lips, black hair and white skin. He is so completely enraptured that he absent-mindedly swipes several attackers from their saddles without even looking up. Later on, in the episode where he arrives at the Grail Castle and fails to ask the important question, he does so out of a curious mixture of politeness and absentia.

It is this which constitutes much of Perceval's success. His chivalry is both of this world and the other: he is a bridge *between* the worlds, able to see into the mists and mysteries of the Faery realm as well as into the harsher realities of daily life.

And this is indeed a most important function of the would-be Grail seeker. To be able to relate the realms of the everyday and the otherworldly into some kind of unity is to move close to the central mystery of the Grail, the ability of which to do the same thing in non-finite terms is one of its greatest gifts. To have one foot in both worlds, the infinite and the mundane, is a blessed state and one which only the truly innocent generally attain.

One could even say that it is necessary to learn how to become truly 'foolish' before one can begin the Quest, for as long as we are enamoured of the 'serious reality' offered by the outside world, we can hardly begin to step outside ourselves in the manner necessary to perceive the Grail. Perceval's ability to do just this makes him a worthy successor to the line of the Grail Kings, and thus, after the achievements of Galahad and the temporary withdrawal of the mystic vessel, he is to be found once more entered into the Castle of the Grail. Here he takes up the role of the Fisher King until such time as a new seeker arrives with the keys of innocence and experience in his or her grasp – at which time Perceval, like his forebears, will step down, leaving the position open to the next initiate.

BORS

For various reasons there has been a tendency to overlook Bors in discussions of the successful candidates. He is generally considered the least romantic of the three, and as Lancelot's cousin lives always in the shadow of his more famous sibling. Also, he is the only one of the three who is actually married, with a child, at the time of the Quest. (Perceval marries later, when the Quest is over.) But Bors thus understands the nature and mystery of human love, of desire and procreation, in a way that neither of his companions ever can.

He is, then, *in* the world where they are only *of* it. This gives him a special degree of insight into the mystery as a whole which makes him the natural choice to be the one who returns to Camelot after the Quest is over, to relate all that has happened to Arthur and the rest of the world.

Bors, then, represents *earthly* chivalry, where Perceval stands for unearthly and Galahad for purely spiritual chivalry. He is the ordinary man whose aims are neither so high nor so lofty as his companions, but who is nonetheless raised by the power of the Grail to a position from which he may witness and experience the greater mysteries. As the poet Charles Williams put it:

> Malory . . . does not say he was married. But he does say that he has a son by another Elayne (not the Grail Princess) . . . . But if we allow Sir Bors his marriage and his work in the world and his honest affections, see how perfect the companionship of the

three lords becomes! There is the High Prince (Galahad), wholly devoted to his end in the Grail; and there is Perceval with his devout and selfless spiritual sister; and there is Bors with his wife and child. These are functions each of the others. The High Prince is at the deep centre, and the others move towards him; but also he operates in them towards the world. These are three degrees of love. Their conclusion is proper to them . . . Bors returns to Camelot, joins Lancelot, is made king, goes on a crusade, and in the last sentence of [Malory's] book dies . . . 'upon Good Friday, for God's sake'[90].

To carry this a step further, we may see the three knights as aspects of Christ. Bors is 'He that has come to bear witness to the truth', to the mystery itself; Perceval is 'He upon whom the Mystery shall be founded'; while Galahad, quite simply, undergoes the great transformations of the Grail in a manner that is the nearest any human being can come to sharing in the Crucifixion and Resurrection of the body. When he first goes aboard the Ship of Solomon, which is to carry him to the country of the Grail, he lies down on the bed made from the wood of the true Cross, thus emulating Christ in symbolic fashion even before he comes to the celebration of the mysteries at Sarras.

Bors, the witness, the 'man in the street', watches and observes everything with a kind of open mouthed wonder, almost bewilderment. He does not know why he has been chosen, or not even what he has been chosen for – yet he accepts, willingly, and treads the path of the Grail along a road which is often far harder for him *because* he is less spiritually-oriented than his fellows.

For this reason perhaps, his temptations are always more rigorous and produce the most dramatic effects. In Malory for example he is already feeling overwhelmed by being faced with a grim choice – that of rescuing his brother or a lady who was being carried off against her will. Bors had chosen the latter and as a result earns the bitter enmity of his brother. Now he is tested yet further when he comes to a castle where he is gently treated, given food and wine and then introduced to 'the richest lady and the fairest of all the world . . . more richly clothed than ever he saw Queen Guinevere or any other.' She is surrounded by fair ladies of her own who tell Bors that she will have no other man but he to be her champion. But there is more to it than this, for the lady then declares that she has always loved him, will do anything for him, so long as he does her will. But Bors is steadfast.

'Madam' said he, 'There is no lady in the world whose will I can fulfil in this way . . . ' 'Ah Bors', said she, 'I have loved you long for the great beauty I have seen in you, and the great strength I have heard of you, that needs must you lie with me this night, and therefore I pray you grant this to me.' 'Truely' said he, 'I shall not do it by no means.' Then she made such great sorrow as though she would have died. . . . And she departed and went up to a high battlement, and lead with her twelve gentlewomen; and when they were above, one of them cried out: 'Ah, Sir Bors, gentle knight have mercy on us all, and suffer my lady to have her way, for if you do not we must all suffer death by falling from this high tower. . . .' Then Bors looked up, and they seemed all ladies of great estate and beauty, and he had of them great pity, but he counselled himself that it were better for them to loose their souls than that he should loose his. . . . And with that they all fell down upon the earth, and Bors crossed himself . . . and anon he heard a great crying, and he saw neither tower or ladies, or castle, for all had vanished away as though they had never been.' (Malory, Bk XVII. Ch. 12.)[52]

This is, admittedly, an extreme example, and one which hardly puts Bors in a sympathetic light. He seems indeed far more concerned with his own well being than that of the supposed lady and her companions. Yet this is typical of his approach to the wonders and tests which happen to him: he comes to them with a solid, clear-eyed sensibility. He knows what is right with a kind of inner certainty, and he does his best to recognise it.

Such an approach may seem old-fashioned and moralistic; yet it shows a single-minded devotion to the Quest which puts Bors firmly among the three Grail winners because he is virtually *unable* to fail. He is typical of the kind of person who proceeds, steadily and cautiously, towards a goal he or she may be scarcely aware of; who follows the code of 'earthly chivalry' to the letter. He may seem unsympathetic – but then so does Galahad, who often follows the dictates of his faith so blindly that it is to the cost of others. What he, Bors and Perceval ultimately show us is that one has to trust to the inner directives of the Quest whatever the cost, and often without knowing for a long time after if one really did choose wisely. But then, the Quest is not expected to be easy, and neither are the tests which its participants undergo.

LANCELOT

So much for the successful candidates; but what of the two who failed? It is difficult not to feel greater sympathy for these, who seem altogether more human and down-to-earth than their peers. Both, Lancelot especially, aim high, throwing their not inconsiderable abilities into the effort to be Grail winners. Lancelot, according to the Christian tradition in which the texts relating to his failure were written, is a 'fallen' man, one who has become very deeply enmeshed in the glamour of the world, and has allowed an image of human perfection (Guinevere) to supplant the image of God. Thus, his open heartedness, his willingness to set all his earthly desires aside to climb the spiritual heights of the Grail mountain, where the temple of the mysteries is situated, but where so few ever come, is not enough.

Throughout texts such as Malory's *Morte d'Arthur*[52] or the *Queste*[56] this point is laboured again and again. As, for instance, when Lancelot, early on in the quest, comes to a cross road and poses to rest there:

'. . . and so he fell asleep; and half waking and half sleeping he saw come by him two horses all fair and white; bearing between them a litter, in which lay a sick knight. And when he was close to the Cross, he paused. All this Sir Lancelot saw for he slept only lightly. And he heard the knight say: 'O Sweet Lord, when shall this sorrow leave me? And when shall the Holy Vessel come to me, through which I shall be blessed? For I have endured long without committing any evil. . . .' Then Sir Lancelot saw a candlestick with six lights come before the cross, though no one brought it there that he could see. Also there came a Table of silver, and the Holy vessel. . . . And the sick knight sat up and held out his hands and said: 'Fair Sweet Lord, who art here with this vessel, take heed of my need that I may be made whole'. And he went on his hands and knees to the vessel and kissed it, and immediately he was made whole and gave thanks. (Bk VIII. Ch.18.)

All this Lancelot sees but is unable to move or speak, so that he cannot tell if he is dreaming or not. But apparently the sick knight can see something which remains hidden from Lancelot, which enables him to be healed. He then comments to his squire that the knight lying close by (Lancelot) must be a great sinner since he is unable to do homage to the Grail. Then, lacking either sword or helmet of his own he takes Lancelot's, along with his horse, which is a better mount than his own.

'Then Sir Lancelot awoke, and sat up, and considered what he had seen and whether or not it was a dream. And then he heard a voice that said 'Sir Lancelot – more hard than the stone, more

111

bitter than the wood, and more naked than the leaf of the fig tree art thou: therefore go hence and withdraw from this holy place.' (ibid.)

So Lancelot departs, and discovers that his horse, sword and helm are gone, from which he understands that it was no simple dream that he experienced. And he realises that he is too sinful to achieve the Quest because, in his own words: 'All my great deeds of arms, I did for the Queen's sake, and for her sake I did battle were it right or wrong, and never did I battle only for God's sake, but to win worship and be the better beloved.' (ibid.)

All Lancelot's strength has been channelled towards winning greater fame or attracting the attention of Guinevere; of acts done for their own sake or out of love for God he knows nothing. Thus, even when he does attempt an act of selfless goodness for the most honest of reasons, he is struck down.

This adventure takes place late in the Quest – for he does not give up, even though he now doubts his own abilities. Like many before and since he continues his course without hope of success, and thus comes close to achieving his desire. He reaches the very door of the Grail chapel and looks within. . . .

Then looked he to the middle of the chamber and saw a table of silver, and the Holy vessel, covered with red samite and with many angels about it. . . . And before the altar he saw a good man dressed as a priest, and it seemed he was celebrating the Mass. . . . And it seemed to Lancelot that there were three men there, and two put the youngest between the Priest's hands, who lifted him up high. . . . And then Lancelot marvelled that the Priest could hold up so great a load . . . and when none came forward to help him . . . he entered into the chamber and came towards the table of silver . . . and there came a great breath of air, all mixed with fire, which smote him . . . so that he fell to earth and had no power to rise, and lost the power of movement, and of hearing and of sight . . . (Malory, Bk. XVII. Ch. 15.)

Even then, out of a desire to help, Lancelot is not permitted to approach the holy things; good intentions are not enough for the Grail seeker, it is necessary to believe, to an almost terrifying degree, in the Quest itself, and to exclude all other things, however honourable, from the mind.

But Lancelot is given a kind of forgiveness. It is his son, Galahad, who finally achieves the Quest. Indeed it is hard to forget, once one has read it, the description of the meeting of father and son on the mysterious Ship of Solomon, where they are permitted to spend some time together and to talk as father and son should.

From that point onwards one knows that Lancelot will never reach a successful conclusion in his search, but that Galahad is destined to succeed, in some way, for him. And this is surely one of the most astonishing and moving parts in the whole story – for we must remember that Galahad is begotten upon the Grail Princess Elaine through Lancelot's being made to think she is Guinevere! Even out of the depths of Lancelot's fault comes healing, the child who will one day outshine his father in the greatest adventure of all.

GAWAIN

Gawain is a different matter. For him, except in a single version of the Quest story, there is scarcely even the chance of achievement. Yet there is a reason to believe that Gawain was once the original Grail winner, in the time before it became Christianised. Then, as I have shown elsewhere[63] Gawain was the Knight of the Goddess rather than of the Virgin as he later became. This places him in a unique position as one who bridges the gap between the Christian and Pagan images of the Grail, and makes him especially important as a subject for deeper study on the part of modern day questers.

In the version of the story given by Chrétien de Troyes, Gawain does indeed find a way to the enchanted castle where the Grail is kept, but like Perceval before him he fails to ask the question which will set in motion the healing of the Waste Land and the Wounded King. Yet he still achieves more than Lancelot, for he does remark upon the Spear which drips blood which is carried in the Grail procession, and this is sufficient to undo some of the harm done to the land through the striking of the Dolorous Blow.

But Gawain still fails to ask more and is deemed unworthy to succeed further. Instead his quest becomes one for the sword of Judas Maccabeus, or sometimes for that which beheaded John the Baptist. But the sword is always broken, and Gawain's task is to discover how to unite the two pieces of the blade. Only after many adventures is he able to do so. For Gawain's fault is impatience, the kind of behaviour which results, right at the beginning of his career, in his beheading an innocent woman who had begged for his help. Thereafter, perhaps not unrelatedly, Gawain is plagued by women, and gains the reputation of a libertine. Yet this is actually an unfair judgement, since he was also famed for his courtesy towards all women, and through his service to the Goddess saw all aspects of the feminine as representatives of deity.

Time has done a considerable disservice to this great knight, who once occupied a place superior to that of Lancelot, and may well have been the Queen's champion before him. A nephew of King Arthur, he was brave, honest and a great fighter in the cause of right. Yet at some point he fell from popularity, perhaps because of the lingering association with paganism, and thereafter literary judgement relegated him to a subordinate position which he never wholly lost.

Thus in Malory's version we find him, late upon the Quest, riding with Ector de Maris, Lancelot's brother. Both complain that they have met with no good adventures, or indeed seen anything of the wonders and marvels promised at the start of the Quest. They arrive at a ruined chapel and decide to rest there. Both have a dream-vision which tell us a good deal about the nature of their failure and the success of the other three.

> Sir Gawain seemed to come into a meadow full of herbs and flowers, and there he saw a herd of one hundred and fifty bulls, that were proud and black, save for three of them, that were all white, and one had a black spot, but the other two were so fair that they might be no whiter. . . . And the black bulls said, among themselves, 'Let us go forth to seek better pasture', and some went and came again, but they were so thin they could hardly stand; but of the three bulls that were white only one returned. . . . And Sir Ector saw himself and his brother Sir Lancelot getting upon their horses, and one said to the other, 'Let us go seek that which we shall not find'. And then he seemed to see that a man beat Sir Lancelot, and despoiled him and put old and torn clothing on him and set him upon an ass. And so he rode until he came to a well, but when he would have drunk from it, the water sank down and he could get no sustenance. (Malory, Bk XVI. Ch.1–2.)

This is straightforward allegory, and tells of the working out of a prophecy made by Merlin at the founding of the Round Table – that many would search for the Grail but few find it. And when asked how this might be he replied:

> . . . that there should be three white bulls that should achieve it, and the two should be maidens, and the third should be chaste. And that one of the three should pass his father as much as the lion passes the strength of the leopard. (ibid. Bk XIV. Ch. 2.)

Merlin is of course referring to the three successful knights, two of whom, Galahad and Perceval, were considered sinless and virgin, and

Bors, who is chaste but married. Galahad is the lion who surpasses his father the leopard. But of Gawain there is once again no mention.

DINDRAINE

No consideration of the Grail seekers would be complete without some mention of a fourth character, who also made the journey to Sarras with the Grail, and who was with the knights who carried the miraculous vessel to its final destination. This is Perceval's sister, sometimes referred to as Dindraine. Her story is simple and brief. Brought up, like her brother, in ignorance of the world, she joins the three knights on the Ship of Solomon when they already have the Grail on board and are journeying to the Holy City. On the way they stop at a castle where the custom is that any virgin who travels that way must give some of her blood to heal the lady of the castle, who is sick with leprosy. The Grail knights would have defended Dindraine to the death, but she willingly offers her own blood as a sacrifice – for such it becomes with her subsequent death. The lady of the castle is healed however, and we can see here a foreshadowing of the healing actions of the Grail itself.

Much can, and has, been written of this episode. Some have chosen to see it as an allegory of Christian sacrifice[44], others have sought deeper anthropological or psychological meanings in menstrual customs or the right of women to serve at the rite of the Eucharist[61]. It is perhaps more appropriate, in the context of the story, to see her as the embodiment of feminine wisdom, completing the quaternity of Grail winners and representing the ability to create new life.

As a recent commentator has put it, this: 'hints at the inner identity of the woman's menstrual blood, which tells her that she has not yet conceived, with the blood of the wounded Grail King, bleeding because he cannot bring to life the [dead land]'[61].

There is much in the story of Dindraine that is mysterious beyond even the Grail itself, which touches upon the role of the Divine Feminine in the mysteries. It will repay considerable meditation by those who undertake the path to the Grail, and it is of course particularly important in that it demonstrates that the new knights do not have to be male.

THE GRAIL EXPERIENCE

When one has looked at the image from every angle, meditated upon it, read the texts and travelled the inner roads, looked in depth at the way in which the individual knights approached the quest, it is, finally, the individual experience which matters most. No matter whether it is apocalyptic or personal, each encounter is relevant in some way to the work of the Grail in the world. There follow two very different reports of such experiences. It is hoped that these accounts may give an idea of the scope of realisation and healing which can come from working with the Grail.

The first report comes from a young woman who had suffered for most of her life from overshadowing memories of her childhood. Things finally reached crisis point, where she felt no longer able to continue with her life as it then was. What followed is told in her own words.

CASE HISTORY ONE

'Previously I had been to Butleigh, near Glastonbury and had had a very vivid experience. This entailed looking at my whole past with a cold but clear eye. I knew that archetypally this corresponded to looking at the Gorgon's face which might turn me to stone or make me mad. I nearly did go mad because things that had happened to me in my childhood were really horrific. I felt that I was standing at the eye of the storm, the very centre of the Wasteland. I felt absolutely desperate. I also knew that Butleigh was the centre of the Glastonbury Zodiac [see Chapter 1] and thus that it must also be the centre of balance and home of the potential Grail. I felt very strongly that this was a place where all worlds were accessible – the hub of the wheel.

'I could see no way out of my extreme unhappiness but to call upon St Michael as "judger of souls", either to let me die or find the Grail. Being in a way one of the raped Well-Maidens [see Chapter 1], sexually ravaged and also "heart-broken", there was no way out. I was very aware of the reality of the Wasteland, and that I could not even commit suicide in order to rest, as I would take my torment with me.

'I went back to London, and there had a Grail experience of an unusually sustained and vivid kind (for me). I saw the door of a church, which I recognised as being at Eweleme in Oxfordshire. I had visited it several times and always felt it contained a mystery, but had not even thought of it for a couple of years. I went inside, and the interior was full of light. In front of the high altar stood St Catherine ablaze with white and golden light. In one hand she held a white sword, her other rested upon a blazing wheel. Beside her stood St George, in white and silver, but passive. Above St Catherine was suspended a rose cup surrounded by golden light.

'Suddenly a massive black hand smashed through the East window. Instinctively I put a seal on the window, banished the hand and moved the "Grail" away into the centre of the church. I did not understand what it was, and thought of a negative, outside force trying to steal the Grail.

'St Catherine handed me the sword, and I knew this meant that I could use it from then on to defend myself – to keep negative forces away from the Grail. St Catherine pointed to the West end wall. On it was a painting of a green cross with golden drops in the background. I recognised this as the emblem of St Helen – the living cross with drops of honey amber. (Afterwards I found it was also the emblem of Joseph of Arimathea.) At the centre of the cross was a rose, which I knew was also the heart of the Grail. Then the black hand smashed through the wall again and grasped the rose.

'I tried to understand what this meant, and decided it must be a symbol of dark, archaic forces, so must be accepted and acknowledged rather than banished. As soon as I had mentally done this, the black hand divided into two, which cupped the rose. Then a dove flew out and upwards and the wall-painting changed so that it now depicted a withered, blackened tree. I knew this was a symbol of me and my life; that my roots, both in this incarnation and in many past ones, were rotten; that rather than heal the "rape", I had attracted the same pattern again and again, thus doing more damage.

'I can't remember quite what I did next. Somehow I mentally released the negativity, made an affirmation of willingness to change. At one point I remember the church door opening and faery people coming in, one in the form of a badger which dug out the roots of the blackened tree. The whole wall then crumbled and fell down, revealing a green, flowering tree behind.

'Then I was outside in the churchyard, sitting on the grass, earthing myself. All around me were animals and faery people. I felt at home, released.

'Two days later a friend told me that "death had gone from my face" and that there was now "a Grail in my heart". I saw the experience as meaning that I do still have a potential chance of happiness and love which I did not have before, rather than some great spiritual achievement. I remembered seeing my own right hand as black for the last few months, and had been worried that I was going to get a disease or that it would somehow be damaged. And I remembered drawing a picture of the Lady of the Grail after I had seen a vision of her in the lane behind Eweleme church years ago. She was woman rather than maiden, as usually depicted – fulfilled rather than virginal.'

CASE HISTORY TWO

The next report comes from an experienced practitioner of the inner magical path, who demonstrates in this account how deeply the imagery of the Grail can strike, and how much can be learned from it.

'In the Spring of 1983 I undertook a series of meditations which took the form of colloquies with an Inner guide. After the dialogue stage came the envisioning. As anyone who has ever meditated will know, this last process is often stubbornly non-productive and boring.

'On 19 March, the day of this particular meditation, I was aware of St Joseph of Arimathea, who shares with St Joseph the Carpenter, this feast-day in the church's calendar. St Joseph of Arimathea is credited with bringing the Grail, or rather more traditionally, two cruets containing the blood and sweat of Christ: the "blood and water", which came from his side at the crucifixion when his side was pierced by Longinus' spear.

'The image was drawn into the meditation wherein I was told that "we must combat the unleashed wildness in the blood". With these words came a picture of chaotic upheaval, of presumptuous pride and unregenerate influences. In short, I was aware of a video of the Fall of Atlantis running in my head. This event, whether one sees it as a mythical or historical happening, lies behind the esoteric tradition as the great admonitory story, just as the Judaeo-Christian Fall is at the basis of orthodox spirituality as a reminder that we continually fail to take responsibility for our actions and must abide the consequences.

'I asked my Inner guide, "How are we to control these influences?" He replied: "Firstly recognise these influences in your own lives. Then transfer them to the receptacle of the Moon Ark of the Grail."

'As I registered these words, I was aware of a feeling so deep, so piercing, that it was as though a child had taken root in my womb. Most mothers will know what this feels like: it is the almost indefinable yet unmistakable presence of life within one's own body. It was a moment as precious to me as the Blessed Virgin's Annunciation by the Angel of the Holy Spirit. The feeling preceded the image of the Moon Ark itself.

'It appeared to me as a pair of hands cupping an orb which pulsed with liquescent, luminous light which was also a singing harmony. I was in no doubt that I was in the presence of the most ancient symbolic appearance of the Grail itself.

'All meditators will testify that such experiences come in a great knot of image, perception, recognition and unfolding which is like a lightening flash of supra-normal comprehension. All artists perceive their creative impulse in a similar way: they see it fully manifest, completely achieved, even though they may not yet have fashioned it with their hands. It was so that the following understandings were clear to me: in a moment of illumination, though the writing down took a little longer.

'The Moon Ark was an energy transformer, a purifer which acted as clearing house for psychic debris. As it had originated in the Moon Temple of Atlantis, which never suffered from the corruption which had sent that mythic civilization plunging to the depths of the sea, it was a vessel of supreme purity. Within this vessel, the life-force, bearing the spark of divinity, could be transferred to each newly-engendered soul. This explained why I felt I had physically conceived. I gathered that this symbol had been ritually used in meditation by priests and priestesses over many generations and that, by virtue of this symbol, they understood the mysteries of engendering. There was nothing sinister or smacking of eugenics about this understanding: theirs was profound guardianship of the seeds of life. And now I had had the same experience, I was changed and charged with purpose. As in the Gnostic teaching story, *The Song of the Pearl*, where the soul takes flesh and descends into incarnation in a series of didactic experiences, so the Moon-Ark was a perfect paradigm of initiation into the spiritual mysteries. As the Platonic form of the medieval Grail, it was a vessel of regeneration more powerful than anything I had ever imagined.

'I meditated upon it frequently over the following months, visualising it as a shallow, crescent-shaped bowl with a round disc hovering over it. I came to see that it was a profoundly simple symbol with staggering implications. As I sat in meditation before its visualised image, the Moon Ark taught me many things. It worked by the power of exchange of energies: whatever went into it came out transformed. It was no good just sitting and looking at it, being totally passive. One had to have an exchange.

'It was Caryll Houselander, a Catholic mystic of the forties, who pointed out that for Christ to work miracles he first of all required the raw material with which to work: using spittle to make paste with which to cure a blind man, an affirmation of regret and repentance in order to heal the afflicted. It is so that the Grail works: Perceval, instructed that it is impolite to ask questions, fails to ask the all-important Grail question by which the Wounded King and the Waste Land will be healed in one stroke, just as they were originally wounded by the Dolorous Blow. The Grail Question is the antithesis of the Spear Which Heals and Wounds. So it is with the Moon-Ark. One must give in order to receive. One must be healed before one can heal others. This is the service of the Grail.'

THE QUEST

Having looked at the nature of the Grail Questers, successful and otherwise, let us now look at the Quest itself as it appears from a contemporary perspective.

It is possible, as has been the case throughout this book, to view the search for the Grail as necessary. It was, after all, active in restoring the Waste Land and the Wounded King, who are really symbols for the wounds in Creation itself, made waste by our inability to understand the Divine purpose. So the argument goes. But we must also be able to see it all in another way – as neither necessary nor indeed desirous. In this way it is possible to see fresh aspects of the stories which may have been obscured by a natural reverence for the subject of the Quest.

So let us not forget that the Quest for the Grail resulted in the deaths of many of its seekers, the humiliation of others; or that it hastened the breaking of the Round Table fellowship by giving its adversaries opportunity to fill the empty places at the Table with their own supporters; and that the Quest ultimately broke the spirit of men like Lancelot and Gawain, so that they were no longer able to resist the tide of darkness which swept in upon them from all sides, and perhaps raged within them as well. For them the Grail was hardly a good thing at all.

Again, Galahad's victory was a purely personal apotheosis; He is able to ascend to heaven, as Malory says 'with a great multitude of angels', while Perceval remains to take up the burden of guarding the Grail, and Bors returns to his old life as though, in some way, nothing had happened. Furthermore, if Perceval does indeed return to the castle of the Grail to become its new warden, then in effect the Quest has been for nothing . . .

This point is raised not to shock but to indicate the different ways in which it is possible to view the Grail Quest, and to show how we may learn something more from a mingling of such approaches. Yes, we can say, the Quest was a failure; it brought destruction in its wake and did nothing for the general good of more than a few people. Or we can look at it another way and say again: the Grail is for all time, and by choosing not to work more than an occasional miracle or so, it leaves the Quest open, a challenge to all who come after.

Obviously the second answer is the one we should prefer. But is it, finally, any more valid than the first? The Grail is a mystery, as few would deny. As one commentator (Joseph Campbell) put it: why should one need to go in search of God (or the Grail) when he was present on every altar of every church in the land?[10] But the Grail is not common only to Christian belief: it is sought, in different guises, in many other parts of the world as we have seen. It is there to be sought, even though it eludes discovery – perhaps until the end of time.

It is time which is important here. It goes with the realisation that there is a right time and a wrong time to go in search of the Grail. Arthur's time, the age of the Round Table, whether we take that as an inner reality or a reflection of the ideals of chivalry, was the wrong time. The apparitions and wonders of the Quest are activated *by the seekers themselves*, as much as by the high powers which control the Grail. Their experience, even their defeat, if such it was, is not wasted. We can learn from it just as we can learn from any great spiritual teaching. Indeed we might think of it as a sublime example from which we can all learn – from both success and failure.

Like all inner impulses – and the Grail, however else we may see it, is most certainly this – it has its own purpose, which we may not always recognise. One aspect only of this may be see in the *transformative* energy of the Grail, its ability to make things other. No one who goes in search of it remains unchanged, and if it had no greater purpose than this it would be sufficient to fulfil its existence.

One further quotation sums up the direction which the Quester sooner or later seems to take. It comes from a Gnostic text, the *Gospel of Thomas*, translated by Gilles Quispel:

Let not him who seeks cease until he finds,
and when he finds he shall be astonished.

It is that degree of astonishment, of surprise, which above all else marks out the Grail mystery. If you have not yet come upon, it is hoped that you will do so, and that it will be as great a reward as you could wish for.

EXERCISE 6: WORKING WITH THE GRAIL

How can we best work with what we learn from the Grail? The exercises throughout this book are designed to promote a direct and personal experience of the mysteries we have been discussing.

They are, however, only a beginning. There are groups throughout the country working with the Arthurian and Grail streams. The present author, together with Caitlin Matthews, gives regular courses every year at Hawkwood College in Gloucestershire, and there are plans to produce a Grail Course in the near future. (For further information write to: BCM Hallowquest, London WC1N 3XX.)

The following exercise is part of a body of received material given at a course for the Wrekin Trust in March 1989.

One of the most basic forms of sickness common to humanity is soul-loss. It is so common that few either know of it nor recognise it. Yet it is a fact that many people are without souls, they have lost touch with their true inner selves. In the same way the earth itself has suffered a wounding through the terrible afflictions which humanity have laid upon it, wounding it in the soul also.

The way towards healing lies first and foremost in the recognition of soul-loss and soul-damage. The Grail can help to restore both of these, on a planetary level and on a personal level. For a planetary level envisage the following: a Grail of light at the centre of the earth, which emits rays forming a penumbra, a soul-envelope around the planet. For personal healing from the Grail, envisage three aspects of the Cup one above the other and superimpose them upon the body. The lowest of the three represents the heart, the middle cup the mind, the highest the soul. When all three are brimming with light, and when the light pours over and irradiates the body, then healing will begin. Finally to unify the two aspects of healing, envisage the Goddess, in whatever form is most pleasing, standing at the centre of a maze of light, holding out her cupped hands which brim with water and light. Approach her and drink from her hands so that you imbibe wisdom, strength and joy from the wells which never run dry. For she herself is a Damsel of the Wells, is **all** damsels of the wells, and she ever continues to offer her Cup to all who are weary from travelling upon the road.

BIBLIOGRAPHY

(All titles were published in London, unless otherwise stated.)

1. Adolf, H. *Visio Pacis: Holy City and Grail* Pennsylvania State University Press, 1960
2. Ancorna, S.G. *The Substance of Adam* Rider & Co., 1934.
3. Ashe, G. *King Arthur's Avalon* Fontana, 1973.
4. Bernard of Clairvaux *On the Song of Songs* Cistercian Pubs., 1976.
5. Bernard of Clairvaux *Treatise in Praise of the New Knighthood* Cistercian Pubs. 1977.
6. Bryant, N. *The High Book of the Grail* D.S. Brewer, Cambridge, 1978.
7. Bryce, D. *The Mystical Way and the Arthurian Quest* Llanerch Enterprises, Llanerch, Dyfed, 1986.
8. Burckhardt, T. *Alchemy* Element Books, 1987.
9. Campbell, J. *The Inner Reaches of Outer Space* Alfred van der Marck Editions, New York, 1985.
10. Campbell, J. *Myths to Live By* Souvenir Press, 1973.
11. Campbell, D. E. Trans. *The Tale of Balain* Northwestern University Press, Evanston, 1972.
12. Cavendish, R. *King Arthur and the Grail* Weidenfeld & Nicholson, 1978.
13. Chrétien De Troyes, *Arthurian Romances* Trans. by D.D.R. Owen. J.M. Dent, 1987.

14. Cooper, J.C. *An Illustrated Encyclopaedia of Traditional Symbols* Thames and Hudson, 1978.
15. Cooper-Oakley, I. *Masonry and Medieval Mysticism* Theosophical Publishing House, 1977.
16. Cross, F.L. *Oxford Dictionary of the Christian Church* Oxford University Press, 1978.
17. Currer-Briggs, N. *The Shroud and the Grail* Weidenfeld & Nicholson, 1987.
18. Day, Mildred Leake, [Ed & Trans.] *The Story of Meriadoc, King of Cumbria* Garland, New York, 1988.
19. De Sede, G. *La Rose Croix* J'ai Lu, Paris, 1978.
20. De Sede, G. *Les Templiers* J'ai Lu, Paris, 1969.
21. De Rougemont, D. *Passion and Society.* Faber & Faber, 1955.
22. Evans, S. *In Quest of the Holy Grail* J.M.Dent, 1898.
23. Fortune, D. *Applied Magic* Aquarian Press, 1962.
24. *The Golden Blade* Issue No. 33. Rudolf Steiner Press, 1981.
25. Gantz, J. Trans. *The Mabinogion* Penguin Books, Harmondsworth, 1985.
26. Gardner, E. *Arthurian Legends in Italian Literature* Octagon Books, New York 1971.
27. Gerald of Wales *Journey Through Wales* Penguin Books, 1978.
28. Geoffrey of Monmouth: *The History of the Kings of Britain* Trans. by Lewis Thorpe, Penguin Books, Harmondsworth, 1966.
29. Geoffrey of Monmouth: *The Vita Merlini* Trans. by J.J. Parry, University of Illinois, 1925.
30. Gogan, L.S. *The Ardagh Chalice* Brown & Nolan, Dublin, 1932.
31. Grossinger, R. (Ed.) *The Alchemical Tradition* North Atlantic Books, California, 1983.
32. Gryffydd, W.J. *Math vab Mathonwy* University of Wales Press, 1928.
33. Gryffydd, W.J. *Rhiannon* University of Wales Press, 1953.
34. Guest, Lady C. *The Mabinogion* John Jones, Cardiff, 1977.
35. Hall, M.P. *Orders of the Quest: The Holy Grail* The Philosophical Research Soc., Los Angeles, 1976.
36. Heinrich von den Tulen *The Crown* Trans. D.W. Thomas, University of Nebraska Press, Nebraska, 1989.
37. Johnson, P. *History of Christianity* Peregrine, 1978.
38. Jung E. & M.-L. Von Franz *The Grail Legends* Hodder & Stoughton, 1971.
39. Karr. P.A. *The King Arthur Companion.* Chaosium Inc., Albany, 1983.

40. Kennedy, B: *Knighthood in the Morte d'Arthur* D.S. Brewer, Cambridge, 1986.
41. Knight, G. *The Secret Tradition in Arthurian Legend* Aquarian Press, 1983.
42. Lacy, N.J. & G. Ashe *The Arthurian Handbook* Garland Publishing Inc. New York, 1986.
43. Lambert, M.D. *Medieval Heresy* Arnold, 1977.
44. Lang-Simms, L *The Christian Mystery* Allen & Unwin, 1981.
45. Lievegoed, B.C.J. *Mystery Streams in Europe and the New Mysteries* Anthroposophic Press, New York, 1982.
46. Lindsay, J. *The Troubadours and Their World* Frederick Muller, 1982.
47. Loomis, R.S. *The Development of Arthurian Romance* N.Y. Norton, 1963.
48. Loomis, R.S. *Celtic Myth & Arthurian Romance.* Columbia University Press, New York, 1927.
49. Loomis, R.S. *Wales & the Arthurian Legend* University of Wales Press, 1956.
50. Macgregor, R. *Indiana Jones and the Last Crusade* Sphere, 1989.
51. Magre, M. *The Return of the Magi* Sphere Books, 1957.
52. Malory, Sir Thomas, *Le Morte d'Arthur* University Books, New York, 1961.
53. *The Mabinogion* Trans. by Lady Charlotte Guest, The Folio Society, 1980.
54. Marie De France, *Lais* Trans. by G. S. Burgess and K. Busby, Penguin Books, Harmondsworth, 1986.
55. Markale, J. *King Arthur King of Kings* Gordon Cremonesi, 1977.
56. Matarasso, P. *The Quest of the Grail* Penguin Books, Harmondsworth, 1969.
57. Matthews, C. *Arthur and the Sovereignty of Britain* Arkana, 1989.
58. Matthews, C. *Mabon and the Mysteries of Britain*, Arkana, 1987.
59. Matthews, C. *Elements of Celtic Tradition* Element Books, 1989.
60. Matthews, J. *An Arthurian Reader* Aquarian Press, 1988.
61. Matthews, J. *At the Table of the Grail* Arkana, 1987.
62. Matthews, J. *Elements of Arthurian Tradition* Element Books, 1989.
63. Matthews, J. *Gawain, Knight of the Goddess* Aquarian Press, 1990.

64. Matthews, J. *The Household of the Grail* Aquarian Press, 1990.
65. Matthews, J *The Grail, Quest for Eternal Life* Thames & Hudson, 1981.
66. Matthews, J. *Taliesin: Shamanic Mysteries in Britain and Ireland* Unwin Hyman, 1990.
67. Matthews, J. & C. *The Arthurian Tarot: A Hallowquest*, Aquarian Press, 1990.
68. Matthews, J & Green, M. *The Grail Seekers Companion* Aquarian Press, 1988.
69. Matthews, J. and Stewart, R.J. *Warriors of Arthur* Blandford Press, Poole, 1987.
70. Morduch, A. *The Sovereign Adventure* James Clarke, 1970.
71. Morizot, P. *The Templars* Anthroposophical Publishing Company, 1960.
72. Newstead, H. *Bran the Blessed in Arthurian Romance* Columbia University Press, New York, 1939.
73. Oldenbourg, Z. *Massacre at Montsegur* Weidenfeld, 1961.
74. Pearshall, L.B. *The Art of Narration in Wolfram's Parzifal & Albrecht's Jungerer Titurel* Cambridge University Press, 1981.
75. Pultarch, *Moralia* Trans. by F.C. Babbitt. Heinemann, 1957.
76. Rolt-Wheeler, F. *Mystic Gleams From the Holy Grail* Rider, 1945.
77. Runciman, S. *The Medieval Manichee* Cambridge University Press, 1969.
78. Skeeles, D. *The Romance of Perceval in Prose* University of Washington Press, Seattle, 1966.
79. Slessarev, V. *Prester John: The Letter* University of Minessota Press, Mineapolis, 1959.
80. Stein, W.J. *The Ninth Century and the Holy Grail* Temple Lodge Press, 1989.
81. Steiner, R. *Christ and the Spiritual World, and The Search for the Holy Grail* Rudolph Steiner Press, 1963.
82. Stewart, R.J. *The Prophetic Vision of Merlin* Arkana, 1986.
83. Stewart, R.J. *The Mystic Life of Merlin*, Arkana, 1986.
84. Topsfield, L.T. *Chrétien de Troyes: A Study of Arthurian Romance.* Cambridge University Press, 1981.
85. Travers, P.L. *What the Bee Knows* Aquarian Press, 1989.
86. Walker, G.B. *Diffusions* The Research Publishing Co. 1976.
87. Waite, E.A. *The Holy Kabbalah* University Books, New York, 1972.
88. Ware, K. *The Orthodox Church* Penguin Books, 1963.

89. Weston, J.L. *From Ritual to Romance* Doubleday, New York, 1957.
90. Williams, C. *The Descent of the Dove* Faber & Faber, 1939.
91. Wilson, I. *The Turin Shroud* Gollancz, 1979.
92. Wolfram von Eschenbach *Parzival* Trans. by A. Hatto, Penguin Books, Harmondsworth, 1980.

Index